<u>Investing for Beginners:</u>

This Book Includes:

- *Swing Trading Strategies Volume 1*

- *Swing Trading Strategies Volume 2*

- *Stock Market Investing For Beginners*

- *Options Trading*

Swing Trading Strategies:

Learn How to Profit Fast with These 4 Simple Strategies

Table of Contents

Additionally, the information in the following pages is intended only for informational purposes and should thus be thought of as universal. As befitting its nature, it is presented without assurance regarding its prolonged validity or interim quality. Trademarks are mentioned without written consent and can in no way be considered an endorsement from the trademark holder.

Introduction

Congratulations on downloading *'Swing Trading Strategies: Learn How to Profit Fast with These 4 Simple Strategies'* and thank you for doing so.

Many people view swing trading as more of a fundamental approach to investing in the stock market. Unlike with day trading where positions are never held for more than a single day, swing traders can conceivably hold their positions for up to several days or even a week or more; some may even hold them for a month.

Still, this is not a clear picture of what swing trading actually is. It is a form of trading that sits right in the center of two other popular trading mechanisms, day trading, and trend trading. The day trader needs to make super-fast decisions and may only hold his assets for a few seconds before selling. Trend traders, on the other hand, are usually in the market for the long haul. They could conceivably hold their trades for months at a time. Swing trading is a blend of these two very different trading styles.

To be successful as a swing trader, it is important to know how to choose the right stocks to invest in. Ideally, you'll want to look for large-cap stocks, which tend to be the most actively traded on most exchanges. In this book, you'll learn how to ride the waves in one direction and know when to get off and collect your rewards at the end.

In the following pages you'll learn:

- How to develop the mind of the trader

- The 'Sector Rotation' strategy

- How to use the 4-hour chart

- What to do with trading fakeouts

- How to execute momentum trading

There is a lot you can learn before you even get started. Keep in mind that no one knows everything there is to know about trading the markets so see this as your first book among many. Here we hope to lay the groundwork from which you can then catapult yourself into a whole new world of profits and hopefully to a whole new way of making a living. With that said, let's get started.

Happy Trading!
There are plenty of books on this subject on the market, so thanks again for choosing this one! Every effort was made to ensure it is full of as much useful information as possible, please enjoy!

Chapter 1: The Mindset of a Trader

There is a good reason why trading is not for everyone. Statistics show that the majority of those who attempt a career in trading is not successful. This leaves us with a burning question...what is the cause of so many failures? Is it because they lack experience? Is it because of the intensity of the trade itself? Or is it because they don't have the right knowledge?

The answer is probably yes to all of those and the answer could also be no. Every day, thousands of traders enter the market; some win and some lose. We all know exactly what happens when we win and make a pretty good windfall, but how we react when we lose is another matter entirely.

Ask yourself, what do you do when you lose or make a poor investment choice? Some people may get discouraged, blame their losses on the volatility of the market and declare it as a waste of time. Another may also get discouraged and want to quit but, the next day they somehow find a renewed experience and are ready to try again. But the true trader will see the loss as a reason to ask more questions and do more research. Yes, they will be disappointed by their losses but, rather than let that loss be a stumbling block, they will use it instead as a stepping-stone. They will view it as an opportunity to revisit their data, reevaluate their position and find out what went wrong. In essence, they will use it as a learning opportunity and see it as becoming a better trader in the future.

Yes, the loss may have been a result of a lack of knowledge, limited experience, or even just bad decisions but, in a trader's mind, the reason for losing a trade is not as important as how they react to that loss.

To be able to do that, a good trader must learn how to keep their personal feelings completely out of the trading process. When you are emotional, it can taint your perspective of trading and affect your judgment. Traders must have an almost mechanical approach to every decision they make.

While all traders are in it for the money, the best ones are in it for the thrill of the game. They are not just following the charts to see whether they are going up or down but, are equally interested in perfecting their skills of analysis with every decision they make. They view everything as a real learning process.

When you trade you must make decisions quickly and be willing to stick to them and follow through with everyone. Each time you look at the charts, graphs, stocks, and other data, you may have only seconds to decide to get in or out of the market, there is absolutely no time for emotional involvement.

This means you need to be mentally stable, but many would be surprised to learn that you also need to be in good physical condition as well. They do not understand that good physical conditioning can actually support your mental acuity. Eating well, getting good physical exercise, and maintaining healthy habits actually supports your mental faculties, which could easily impact your choices when it comes to making good trading decisions. People who have poor health may not realize how their physical condition could have an adverse effect on their decision-making process.

Trading is more than the ability to watch the numbers going up and down on a graph, it's about the psychology behind those numbers. All those squiggly lines, bars, and shapes represent decisions that individuals make to enhance their interest in a particular stock so the trader must have the ability to get into the minds of others and predict what he or she expects the majority of people will do. Then the trader needs to determine where he or she will best fit in that picture and make their decisions accordingly. At the same time, a trader must also create an escape hatch that will help them to get out of a trade to cut their losses whenever a decision he or she makes goes wrong.

The mind of the trader must be able to handle stress as well. It is difficult to watch the rise and fall of the market and realize that you missed your window to get in or out at the right time. One bad decision in this regard could really ruin your life in the future. It is said that patience is a virtue but, it can also be a lifesaver for the truest and most successful traders.

Just as you would work to hone your physical body, the best traders also put a lot of energy in developing their skills and sense of discipline. The more you practice in this area, the easier it will be. The ability to identify a good stock, learning how to time the market, and predicting price movements are just the public demonstration of the psychology behind the art of trading.

You also must be willing to be a lifelong learner. When it comes to navigating the many instruments you can trade in, you will always find that there is something else you need to learn. This means you must have humility and be willing to openly admit when you don't know something. The moment you become over-confident and think you've mastered a certain skill you can pretty much bet that something will come along to knock you back down a peg or two. You'll either lose your shirt or you'll be beating yourself up for a missed opportunity.

There is a very specific art to swing trading and learning everything you can about the market is tricky. Being able to do a proper analysis and make the right decisions is only a reflection of what's going on in your own personal mindset. To be a good trader, one that is successful most of the time, depends on how well your mind works and how well you know and understand people. Every trade you make will be a reflection of that mental acuity that you have developed. If you for any reason that feel you are weak in this regard, don't despair. It just means that now is the time to start sharpening your tools so you're ready to get the best that you can possibly get out of your trades.

How to Find Potential Trades

One of the most important factors in successful trading is mastering the ability to choose the right instruments to the trade. Many do not realize that there is also a certain psychology to making the right choice. It is just as important to identify not just those stocks that will move, but also where to look for them. No matter how good you are at trading if you can't identify the right instruments to trade you won't get very far as a trader. You need to be able to identify those stocks that have enough movement to generate a profit for you and those that have the volume to match it.

When choosing a good trading stock, it is not enough to pick something you just like and can get excited about, but you must also be able to put your personal feelings aside and focus solely on the numbers. While a good product is definitely a plus, much more is involved in choosing the right stock. You want to see more than a movement, you must also be able to identify the direction its next move will be. To do this, you should look for those stocks that have a strong risk/reward ratio.

You can identify these stocks of the current news items circling around them, their numbers will show them, usually moving up or down more than 2% even before the market opens, and they generally have a lot of unusual premarket activity to go along with it.

Keep in mind that not all stocks are ideally suited for trading so as a trader you will need to be willing to evaluate them on a case-by-case basis. Just because a stock has a high trade volume does not necessarily mean that it is a good choice for swing trading and the fact that it has a low trading volume does not preclude it from consideration. Only after careful analysis can you determine whether a stock is the ideal trading instrument. You need to look for those stocks that are performing outside of the average to decide if it's the right choice for you.

There are many factors that must be considered when trying to choose the right stock. It is easy to think that you can just go by the books and get the results you want, but that would put you at a disadvantage. The numbers can reveal a great deal about a particular stock, but sometimes just relying on your human instinct can be a better gauge for making the right choice or even knowing just where you should look to find the right stock for your next trade.

Making the right choice will depend on a combination of your personal knowledge of the market, the skills you have honed to perfection and your natural instinct. Missing any one of those factors could definitely cause a major problem for anyone looking to get into swing trading.

Chapter 2: The Sector Rotation Strategy

One of the most effective strategies in swing trading is sector rotation. It has been proven to be an excellent means of generating profits with the least amount of risk. There are a few things you must keep in mind when you're practicing sector rotation:

- Market Timing — when the market is going down to avoid buying any stock. This includes purchasing any type of ETFs or sector funds.

- You will divide the market up into specific sectors. Some of these sectors will perform better at different times than at other times.

- Evaluation of each sector using both technical and fundamental analysis.

- Rotate the sectors every month to capitalize on your profit potential.

We'll go through each of these phases in more detail in the next section.

The general idea behind sector rotation is that each sector may perform differently depending on the time of the year it is. So, while some sectors may perform well in the spring others may have their time in the limelight in the summer or winter seasons.

Your goal is to identify those stocks and when you have the best chance of generating a profit from them. To do this, you will need to break down the different stocks into sectors first and do a detailed analysis of each sector. Once you've chosen the sector you want to trade in, you will have to do a separate analysis of each stock within that sector to narrow down your options for trading.

There are a number of websites that are perfect for listing the different sectors and the stocks contained in them. For a quick reference, you can go to Finviz.com to get a listing of the ones that are performing the best. However, if you are just beginning, it may be better for you to do the analysis and ranking yourself so that you can get a better feel for how they are divided up.

The general gist of sector rotation is being able to move your money from one industry to the next in an attempt to glean the most out of the market at any given time. As you go through the different industries, it is important to keep in mind that the past performance of any particular stock is not a guarantee of future success. With that thought in mind, there are four different stages of market movement you must understand.

- **Market Bottom:** This is the point where the prices of a particular stock begin to decline, creating an all-time low.

- **Bull Market:** This is when the market begins to rally and come back to life.

- **Market Top:** This is the point when the market reaches its maximum potential and begins to flatten out.

- **Bear Market:** This is when the market starts its long trip to the market bottom.

There are also four stages of the economic cycle that are important to always keep in mind. Remember that these cycles usually trail behind the market cycles by at least a few months.

Full Recession

When there is a full recession, it can be a difficult time for many businesses. The country's GDP will have been retracted for several quarters, interest rates will have dropped, and consumer expectations will have seriously declined. There are few industries that fare well during this period of time, however, those that are cyclical tend to do better. The technology industry and industrial markets also seem to do well in this type of economic climate.

Early Recovery

In this phase, things are beginning to improve economically. Consumers will begin to expect more from the market and industrial production is starting to see a gradual increase. By this time, interest rates have already bottomed out and aren't expected to fall any further, and the yield curve (the line that plots the interest rates used as a benchmark for measuring the economic climate) is starting to rise. Industries that tend to do better in this type of economic cycle are usually the industrial sector, those that supply basic materials, and towards the end of this cycle, you might even see potential in the energy sector.

Late Recovery

During this economic phase, you will see a rapid increase in interest rates and the yield curve will begin to flatten out. Consumer expectations will begin to drop, and the industrial industry will level off. Industries that fare better during this phase include energy, staples, and services.

Early Recession

During the earlier recession, things will begin to decline for everyone. This is a period when consumer expectations will fall to an all-time low, the production industry will start to fall, and interest rates will be at their highest. The yield curve will neither be rising or falling but instead will remain flat or maybe inverted. The industries most likely to perform well in this economic climate will be services, utilities, cyclical, and transports.

In most situations, financial markets will try to predict the economic climate in the future. They may make predictions as far ahead as six months, putting the market cycle ahead of the economic cycle. So, when you hear news reports about the economic condition of a particular stock it may be well ahead of the current situation. So, a stock may be struggling at the time, but the news reports may already be talking about its recovery.

This gives you a pretty basic understanding of how the different sectors can be divided up and how to choose which ones will be best suited to trade. Even with this basic overview, you can quickly determine which industries are most likely to succeed during the different stages of the economic cycle. Once you've determined which market cycle and economic cycle you're in, it will be much easier to determine which companies you are more likely to take a risk on and give you a better chance at earning a profit.

There are two different ways you can earn profit through sector rotation. First, you can buy when the sector is trending upward and sell when the trend is beginning to fall backward. This is a basic rule of thumb, buy low and sell high. This concept is pretty easy to understand, but it is not always easy to detect. If you're like most people who enter the market, deciding when a price has hit its peak so you know when to get out is not always easy. The same can be said for determining the point at which the price has hit its lowest point possible.

If you're not completely sure how to go about it, there are several free websites you can refer to that will give you their viewpoint on whether the price is maxed out or not. Whatever you do, it is not a good idea to guess at what stock will perform well. Flash crashes are quite common and to be forewarned is to be forearmed.

You can also use charts to predict market movements. Beginners usually will start with something simple like the Simple Moving Average (SMA) to help them to make their decisions. Listed below are a few ways you can use to help you decide which way to go.

Identifying the Bottom of a Sector

It is difficult to determine when a sector has reached the bottom or the top of its cycle. However, if you choose to use the SMA-350, (that's the Single Moving Average over 350 sessions) to determine the market you could probably get a pretty good picture of when the market will begin to make its next dive.

18

Historically, stock prices have generally been seen to hit bottom after six months into a recession. As we've already pointed out, once several quarters have closed the negative growth of the GDP is a strong indicator. However, identifying these periods is not always that easy to see. Usually, if you rely on the six-month in a pattern most of the action has already taken place. As the expression goes, hindsight is always 20/20. However, there are other strategies that can actually be very useful when it comes to detecting a bottomed-out stock.

Nothing could be better than getting into the market when a stock has reached its bottom point. That's when you can buy at the lowest possible prices and then ride the wave all the way to the top. To do that, you just have to watch and observe the averages before it reaches that point. If the averages have experienced a large break that falls below the previous low, it is a signal that you need to follow that stock and observe what happens next. There are several things that can happen. If the average experiences some type of reversal it could be an indication that a double bottom is developing.

You can also keep a close eye on the stock's volume. This measures the amount of activity going on with that stock; which is basically how much buying and selling is actually happening. If you observe a heavy volume going either up or down it is an indication that the buyers and sellers have a pretty strong conviction. If there is a lot of volume moving up, then there is strong support from buyers and if you see a lot of volume moving down it indicates that there is a great deal of support from sellers.

Looking at economic numbers can also tell you a great deal about a stock. The market will experience a decline after the negative news reports appear in the media. You need to think of the press as a reflection of the psychology of the moment. When you begin to see repeated headlines discussing how bad the economy has become, it is usually a sign that the majority of people have developed a very negative attitude towards the market and many investors will be moving out of their positions running for a safer haven as a result.

Consumer Confidence Index

Right after the market has bottomed out, consumer spending will begin to increase showing that consumer confidence has improved. This can be observed when they begin to spend more money and businesses start to see an increase in their earnings.

Managers' Index

This measures the economic health of a sector. When the consumer's confidence index and the manager's index both have hit rock bottom they will begin a steady rise that will continue for several months. You'll usually see this when you're observing the movements of the manufacturing and service sectors and indicates that they are beginning to expand and grow again.

High Yield Bonds

The high yield bond spread consists of bonds from companies who are at a high risk of default. To draw investors that they can borrow from, they will offer to pay a higher interest rate as an incentive. When the usual lending standards begin to relax you will notice the amount of interest for these types of loans will start to drop. This is a sign that banks and other financial institutions are prepared to take on more risk showing that the economic conditions are beginning to improve.

Copper Prices

Many will also look at how the price of copper is moving. It is usually a good measure when showing the strength or weakness of the overall economy. Since copper is so widely used in products like pipes, radiators, electronics, and other technological devices, observing how its price moves are a pretty good measure in determining consumer demand. If you notice that the price has bottomed out, then you can pretty much determine that the demand for those products is also pretty low. However, if there is still room for the price to drop further it's a good chance that there is still some demand for the production of many of the products that use copper.

Ideally, you want to enter the market when the prices have reached the bottom and are starting to climb upward again. It means that there is an increase in demand and prices are about to rise once more.

Being able to identify a market bottom is a key factor for any trader. It requires looking at a variety of different factors that involve both technical analyses as well as understanding the psychology of the masses. You could choose to rely entirely on the numbers, but you would only be cheating yourself. However, when you use all the different indicators you can unlock the key to a host of profit potential.

Detecting the Trend

Another strategy you can use in sector rotation is detecting the trend. Sometimes this can be much easier than identifying the top or the bottom of a market cycle. Some traders use the metric SME-50 (50-day Single Moving Average). Here if you see the stock price has moved up more than 3% above the SMA-50 it is a good time to buy in, but if you see the price has dropped more than 3% below the SMA-50 that's when it is a good idea to sell.

Of course, once you get the hang of this type of analysis, you can always adjust your metric. You don't need to stick to the 3% threshold and may prefer to use 1% or 2%. The key is to find a measure that will work best for you. Generally, if you plan to hold your stocks for a longer period of time, it is better to use a higher percentage and if you plan to sell after only a short period of time, use a lower percentage. You should also adjust your formula to reflect the frequency of the trades you want to make as well.

Identifying market crashes are also important. This tells you when it's a good time to get back into the market. There are also several indicators to help you to determine this as well.

The RSI (14) is a measure showing whether or not a stock has been overbought or oversold. The RSI usually oscillates between 0 – 100. A stock is considered to be overbought when the value increases to above 70 and it is oversold if the measured value is below 30.

What Should You Buy

Now that you have a good idea of when to get into the market and the type of market you want to trade you're only halfway there. In each industry, there may be hundreds, if not thousands of stocks to choose from so narrowing down your search for a good stock can be a little tricky. The stocks you choose will depend on a number of varying factors, some may be within your control and others may be out of your powers of influence.

You will have to consider your level of experience, and the amount of capital you want to invest. The method you chose to try to pick your stocks should be a part of your permanent trading plan and should be adjusted as your experience and knowledge in this field grows. Keep in mind that stocks will have different levels of price movements and velocity. Some will move very slowly, and others will move very quickly. All of these factors will help you to decide which is the best choice for you.

Before you even begin to choose stocks, however, it is important for you to determine the kind of risk exposure you can handle. Your strategy should be created with this foremost in mind. You want to reduce the amount of capital at risk and limit your exposure, but at the same time, you want to earn a sizable profit. The best way to accomplish that is to make enough, right decisions that you can generate a steady stream of profit for yourself.

Keep your process simple. Whatever strategy, it is that you're using start by trading a single stock and then sit back and observe what happens. Every stock has its own personality and habits. The more you understand them the easier it will be to anticipate its movements. Look at the charts at different times throughout the day to determine when it moves and how it responds to external stimuli. Think of it as developing a love interest. You want to know all its little quirks and habits. In time, your relationship will solidify, and you'll be able to predict its movements with surprising accuracy. You won't get it right every time, but the number of wrong predictions will eventually begin to diminish. Once you've reached a level of consistency, you can move on to get to know other stocks in your particular industry.

One important thing you need to remember. Once you've started a trading plan, do not change it while you have a stock in play. Once you've pulled out and the market is closed, you can then look back and make some adjustments to your plan. This way you will know the exact results of your decision and you'll get a clearer picture of whether or not your trading strategy is really working or not.

For the beginning, an investor should remember these basic guidelines.

- Pick a maximum of 50 stocks to trade, but invest them 1 at a time until they become second nature to you

- Choose the low stock prices, but not at the bottom, make sure they are at least above the $25 range

- Look for an average 30-day volume that is higher than 500,000 shares per day

- 25 of your shares should be set aside for long investments

    o They should show increasing revenues and earnings
    o Have a strong presence in their sector
    o Have a moving average around 200
    o Could even be following S&P Futures

- 25 of your shares should be used for short-term investments

    o These should show declining revenues and earnings
    o Have a weak presence in their sector
    o Have a moving average below 200
    o Could be following S&P Futures

Some Sectors That Have Been Favorable for Swing Traders

- Retailing

- Automotive

- Housing

These industries usually suffer when the interest rates are very high, however, when the economy begins to improve these industries will quickly recover.

You can also look at sectors based on the economy. Those in foreign countries will respond to different factors. You will have to consider currency fluctuations, political climate, and favorable or unfavorable events in the news.

When to Rotate

Once you have your sector choices for the market timing, you will need to know when to get out and switch to another sector. There are several methods to help you to decide exactly when it's the best time to rotate.

- When the market is on a downward slope

- When the fundamentals of your chosen sector start to go bad

- When you can find another sector with a higher potential for appreciation

- When you see that the sector is peaking and has met your target objectives

Top-Down Investing

With top-down investing the approach is a little different. You must look at the overall economy and then break down each of its components into smaller details. This means getting a good look at the global world scene, you can examine the different industrial sectors and choose those that have the potential of outperforming the market.

To do this you can use the macroeconomic variables like the trade balances, GDP, currency movements, inflation, and interest rates to help you to narrow down which sectors are most likely to be high performing.

Many investors get this information from hosted forums like the UBS CIO Global Forum held in Beverly Hills, California in 2016 to help them navigate the current economic environment. These venues address many of the macroeconomic factors that investors need to know. Open discussions on international governments, central banking, differing monetary policies, and what's happening in international companies can all have an influence on how a sector is responding into the market.

List of Sectors You Might Want to Consider

- Consumer Discretionary

- Consumer Staples

- Energy

- Financial (including banks, insurances, and brokers)

- Health Care (including pharmaceuticals)

- Industrial

- Material

- Technology

- Utilities

- Automotive

Each of these sectors can be subdivided into even smaller sector groups.

Now that you have all of your information together, you can now narrow down your search and determine which sectors you will trade in when you plan to trade, and which stocks you will focus the majority of your interest in. Sector rotation sounds very simple here, but there are many factors that must be considered if you want to make this type of investment strategy profitable for you.

Chapter 3: The 4-Hour Chart

Using the 4-hour chart are another popular method often used by swing traders. There are quite a few good reasons why working with this chart is so appealing. First, it is a bit longer than the smaller 5-minute or 15-minute charts that do not give a full enough picture of what's really happening with the money. But it is just long enough for investors to get a pretty good picture of what's kind of movement is going on in the market. By using this type of chart, it is pretty easy to see just who is in control at any given time, the bears or the bulls.

With the 4-hour chart strategy, the idea is to tap into the prevailing trends and make the most out of them by using a combination of several different moving averages, support or resistance, volatility, and other tools. When used together, these can help you to maximize your profits while at the same time keep your losses down to a minimum.

With the 4-hour chart as your base, you can screen for potential areas where you might find trading signals. Your main goal here is to identify either an uptrend or a downturn and then follow its unique behavior.

This is usually done by using two different sets of moving averages; one will be a 34 period and the other will be based on the 55 periods. These are both numbers that can be found in the Fibonacci sequence. You will be able to determine if a trend is good for trading or not by analyzing the relationship between the price action and the moving averages.

To Determine the Uptrend

You will be able to identify an uptrend if you have observed any of the following conditions

- The price actions are higher than the two moving averages

- The price action remains above both moving averages

- If the 34-moving average is higher than the 55 moving average and remains high

- If the moving averages are sloping upward for the majority of the time on the chart

To Identify a Downtrend

For there to be a downtrend, the same conditions must be observed, but in the opposite direction.

- When the price action falls below the two moving averages

- The price action stays below the two moving averages

- The 34-moving average is lower than the 55 moving average and remains low

- The moving averages are on a downward slope for the majority of the time and continue to fall behind the trend

Your goal is to profit on the swings that follow in the direction of the trend. This means you must also look for retracements and enter the market at that point. Below are some basic guidelines that can help you to decide the best point to enter the market.

- A trend must be identified in the 4th hour with the moving averages meeting the criteria listed above.

- Wait for a retracement to begin and then watch for the price to move in the direction of the two moving averages.

- When you see the retracement has reached the area between the two moving averages, look at the 1-hour chart of possible entry points.

- Find the retracement trendline that is moving counter to the trend and has touched the trend line at least three times.

- In the 1-hour chart, look for a breakout where a retracement trendline has closed in the same direction as the larger trend.

- Enter when the breakout price closes past the trendline.

One of the advantages of this strategy is that the trends are much more easily identified on the 4-hour chart. In most charts the upswings will be seen with white, rising candles and downswings can be seen with black, falling candles. It should be pretty easy to see the difference.

As a swing trader, you need to be able to visualize these movements and compare them to the current market situation. This strategy works best when there is an up or down trend but will work even when there is a sideways trend.

There is a bit of psychology involved this trading strategy too. When the market experiences a certain level of support, there are many buyers hanging on the sidelines just waiting to jump in at the moment it moves up or down. As a trader, it is important that you can identify the psychological marks and predict when others are prepared to join the party.

Timing

The 4-hour chart also makes it easier to figure out the right time to enter or exit the market. When it comes to swing trading, in addition to getting the direction right, you need to know when the optimum time is to get in or out. As a matter of fact, timing plays a major factor in how well you do.

You also need to be concerned about periodic counter movements. At times you'll notice the market may run as much as 30-50 points against your position, but you will still make a profit if you stay your course. This is one advantage that a swing trader has over a day trader, who could never afford those types of counter movements.

Swing traders can also turn a much larger profit for each position they take. Chances are you are more likely to gain the most profit from those unexpected movements rather than those you predicted. With this method, you will typically have several hours to decide on a specific entry point, so you can afford to wait until you've found the perfect time to take your position.

Setting your Stop-Loss Placement

While this is a very profitable way to make money with swing trading, it is not without risks. Therefore, it is very important that each time you set your position you also create your own stop-loss placement carefully. This will help you to reduce your exposure risk and keep you from bleeding money when things go wrong.

Stop-loss placement is not the most idealistic decision a swing trader needs to make but is likely the smartest. If you do not fully understand how to pick the right position to stop your losses, you stand to suffer considerable consequences. It is the single most powerful weapon needed to manage your risks.

The general theory is that the stop-loss should be based on a specific level in the market. The price action should have breached that level as evidence that your trade was actually wrong. Ideally, you want to see that the price actually invalidated your view and has used fact-based evidence as proof in the form of a breach of support or resistance.

There are several different types of stop-losses you can put into place. They are there as a protection not just for you are losing but to help you to be aware of potential losing trades. There is a tendency, especially among new traders to hold onto losing trades for far too long. We see a price plunging and it is just human nature to hold onto them in hopes that they will rebound, no matter what the conditions really are. By having a stop loss in place, it reduces your exposure to risk and cuts your losses.

Before you can accurately place a stop-loss, you must first answer one question: "At what point is it determined that your trade is wrong?" To answer this, you will need to go back to your analysis, which will tell you not only determine where to place your stop-loss but also what type of stop-loss you will need.

Hard Stop

This is the easiest stop-loss placement you can use. It is just a matter of placing a stop at a certain number of pips from your entry price. A pip is actually the smallest price movement that any exchange can make. So, if a price is set at four decimal places, the smallest change would be that of the last decimal point or $1/100^{th}$ of 1%. This means that you must also factor in the actual movement in the market. More volatile markets will require larger pipes to be effective and less volatile markets will require a smaller number of pips to show that your decision may have been wrong.

Average True Range % Stop

Another type is the ATR% stop, which can be used in any type of market. It is often used to determine the average true range of a particular stock. This range measures the volatility of a stock over a set period of time. When the ATR is higher, it is an indication of a more volatile market, but a lower ATR shows less volatility. Using this measure to determine your stop point is a way of ensuring that your stop will not be static but will be dynamic enough to change with the prevailing market conditions.

Multiple Day High/Low

This type of stop is a popular one for swing traders. When taking a long position, the stop would be placed at the point where the trader will expect the day's low to be. This will allow you to exit the position at the first point where the break below that point is reached.

Closes Above or Below Price Levels

You can also set your stops when the price closes above or below predetermined price levels. With this type of setup, there is no actual stop placed in your trading software, instead, you will have to close it manually when it reaches a specific point.

Which Markets are Best?

When it comes to swing trading, there are certain markets that are much better with the 4-hour chart than others. Shares may be the first choice, but they are not always the most ideal for all traders. There are certain factors that are out of your control that can impact your ability to earn a profit.

For those traders that wish to avoid huge price gaps, the alternative is to trade in specific markets. Rather than focus on particular stocks to invest in, concentrate on a market as a whole. For example, for those who choose to trade the Dow Jones, they are investing in not a single stock but in 30 different companies. So, while a single share may struggle on a particular day it is much more difficult for the entire market to experience a major loss.

This will prevent there being extreme gaps in profit earnings when the markets are very volatile. It is important to point out that there is no guarantee that this strategy won't experience major losses; it simply lowers your overall risk of losses you might experience by focusing your energies on a single stock. So, which markets are the best?

Indices
Bonds
Currencies

When you focus your attention on these, you will see many correlations that you can gauge by following practical rules. For example,

- When the American markets start to rise, markets in the other parts of the world will also see an increase.

- If the US dollar sees an increase, other currencies will often go down

- When the dollar is strong, other commodities are often weakened.

Simply by following these basic rules, you are fully prepared to know when to enter and exit the market and what to expect.

Which Instruments Are Best for Swing Trading?

Exchange-traded funds are investment funds that are traded on an exchange. Even if you don't know anything about these ETFs, there is plenty of information online, so you can learn about the pretty quickly.

The majority of ETF's have a pretty good liquidity, so it should be relatively easy to sell your position when you are ready to exit. Some of the most popular ETFs includes SPT – Standard and Poor's 500, QQQ – NASDAQ, and GLD – Gold.

When you trade on the 4-hour chart you need to develop a good understanding of the different items that you come across when you do your analysis. While you may have already heard of some of these expressions, it is a good idea to review them again so that you start off on the right foot.

When you are searching for a setup (a pattern found on the stock market chart) you need to know what each of these things means. Many of them are very simple and basic but it helps to understand them when you see them and use them in making your investment decisions.

Support and Resistance

Look for support and resistance. These are some of the most powerful characteristics you can find when you're analyzing a market chart. These are usually found when you are doing your technical analysis.

Support is found when a price level appears at the point where the market repeatedly turns upward. This is the point when buyer interest increases. The more buyers in a market the higher the price will be.

Resistance is just the opposite. It is the point when the price level turns downward indicating that there are more sellers in the market. These push the prices down.

The reason why these points are so crucial is that, in some markets, a larger investor will only buy in when the price hits a certain point. While we can't all manipulate the market like this, knowing when these points happen can help you to buy in at the same point and reap the same profits.

As a swing trader, being able to recognize these pivot points could be one of the most profitable strategies you can have at your disposal. It will allow you to buy at the support level and sell at the resistance level for a steady stream of income.

Double Top and Double Bottom

Another pattern you will see on the charts is the double top and the double bottom. The double top pattern can usually be identified by an 'M' on the chart. It is viewed as an indication of an intermediate or sometimes a long-term price reversal. There will be two bullish attempts to push the price up past the resistance levels with two failed attempts to break through the threshold.

This pattern usually appears at the end of a long and extended uptrend. After reaching a specific high, the price will make a significant drop in value and create a trough before another attempt to break through to the new high. The second peak appears to be reaching the first peak but is usually with a lower volume of trade. It's a sign that the bulls have lost confidence in the fight. The price drops again, and the bears will take control.

This is considered to be a bearish chart pattern and is confirmed only when the price breaks at the low point of the trough. Traders can find this by looking for a high-volume breakdown and then enter with a short position to take advantage of the reversal.

Ideally, you want to calculate the distance between the two peaks and the trough and then subtract the result from the lowest point of the trough to find the right point of entry for your trade.

The double bottom pattern is exactly the opposite and can be recognized as a 'W' on the charts. It gives you a good picture of a drop in a particular stock, then an attempt to rebound, followed by another drop to almost the same point before it rebounds a second time.

To trade on a double bottom, the closing price can be found on the second rebound and is almost to the previous high of the first rebound. You'll see an increase in volume combined with the fundamentals that give evidence that the market conditions are in agreement with the reversal. Trade long in this environment and enter at the top of the price point of the first rebound and set your stop at the second lowest.

The best way to trade on a double bottom is to stay abreast of the kind of news that would influence your stock. The more you know about what's going on and what factors are influencing buyer's decisions is to keep on top of the media and make sure that you know what's about to happen before it actually does.

Breakouts

Another pattern you need to be able to identify are the breakouts. These occur when the price moves outside of the support and resistance levels along with a large increase in volume. Those who trade on a breakout position usually enter long right after the stock price breaks above the resistance level. They can enter a short position when the price breaks below the support.

It is important to note that once a breakout occurs volatility tends to increase as the price is moving beyond a known parameter. Breakouts are found in all types of markets and generally represent the most explosive price movements.

When trading on a breakout, keep in mind the support and resistance levels. The more times a stock price has touched on these areas, the stronger these levels become. That means that the longer these areas have been at work, the better the result will be when the price finally breaks.

Choosing your entry point is pretty basic when you're trading with a breakout. Once the price is set to close above the resistance level, you can take a bullish position and when it closes below the support level you can take a bearish position.

Flags

Once a trend movement becomes stronger you will begin to see consolidation on the chart. The market will seem like it has stalled for a short period of time and then it will continue on following the prevailing trend. Sometimes this lack of movement is referred to as a 'trend continuation pattern.' It looks sort like a flag on the charts with the previous uptrend forming the pole and the short bursts of consolidation taking the shape of the flag.

When a flag formation is reached, traders can speculate on whether or not the trend will continue. These are great opportunities for a trader to speculate on both sides. There are bullish as well as bearish flags so there is an opportunity on both sides.

If you can play the flags just right, you can typically earn a pretty good risk-reward ratio. These appear frequently on the 4-hour chart, which makes it the perfect tool to use with this strategy.

Chapter 4: Trading Fakeouts

There is no doubt that talking about the market is much easier than actually doing it. With so many factors to consider it's no wonder that many people end up giving up after a time. Every trader needs their own body of algorithms, formulas, and strategies to help them navigate the sometimes-murky waters of the trading game.

Those new to trading may be surprised to discover that everything you see on a chart is not always as it appears. There are often tricky characteristics that have been manipulated without the best of intentions. These are sometimes referred to as 'fakeouts' or 'feints.' Being able to identify them can be instrumental in helping you to avoid pitfalls and dangers that can easily overtake a newcomer and leave you helpless.

It is true that the same patterns on charts are repeated over and over again. These can usually be identified when you perform a technical analysis, but even then, it may not always be clear.

To avoid being caught in a fakeout it helps to get a clear understanding of what it is. A fakeout (feint) can be described as a situation where the trader takes a position in anticipation of an expected price movement, but that movement never actually happens. Instead, the asset moves opposite of the trader's position.

To avoid this happening, it is recommended that you always use more than one indicator when making trading decisions. As you gain more experience in trading, you'll find that those traders who are most successful even rely on four or more indicators before they commit to a decision.

How to Spot a Fakeout

These fakeouts can occur anywhere, at any time, and in all types of markets so it pays to know just how to spot them when they appear. Below is a list of tips that can help even the beginning trader to identify fakeouts and avoid them.

One of the best ways to identify a true fakeout is by studying the charts of legitimate trends so you can learn how to recognize how price movements really do develop. You'll be able to see this in the candlestick pattern on the chart.

If there is a sudden rise in the market, you should be able to identify only white candles on the chart. Black candles appear when there is a downtrend. In these markets, you'll find that there is a loyal following. With these types of stocks, it is pretty easy to predict movements, so it won't be easy for a large trader to get in and manipulate the prices.

Once the trend has reached its target, the market generally calms down and the volatility decreases. After that, it moves sideways for a period of time. It appears to be meandering aimlessly without forming any clear direction as if it were resting. In this scenario, all traders seem to have come to an agreement on the expected price point.

This scenario usually occurs when there is an expectation of big news relating to the stock. Reports of labor market disputes, major economic changes, or interest rate adjustments can often have a big impact on how the market will perform. It is the trader's responsibility to identify the validity of the movements and if he should anticipate more movement in a specific direction. However, if there is nothing happening in the market, no big news reports on the horizon, or no other indication of a change in price, you should probably assume it is a fakeout.

Traders can manipulate markets easier when there is not a lot of volume going on. They understand that there are many people sitting on the sidelines waiting for a signal for them to jump in and if he has enough money he can set up a fakeout pretty easily and then he can come in and reap the benefits.

By setting up a breakout, for example, traders will easily jump into the fray anticipating a rise in price. However, the trader who initiated the breakout immediately reverses his position once the other traders have joined in, forcing them to close their positions with a loss.

To gain from being trapped in a fakeout, it is better to wait for a breakout and if it ends up being a feint, respond in the opposite direction. Fakeouts usually appear on the support and resistance levels so you should be able to identify and predict certain price movements. Many traders are often caught at this point as it is a common rule of thumb to buy at support levels and sell at resistance levels.

Trading the Fakeout

Once you know how to identify a fakeout, you should prepare a strategy that will allow you to make the most out of the experience. This is what more experienced traders do. Rather than accept a loss as newbies often do, by applying a few basic rules you can turn that potential loss into a possibility for profit.

- Find the consolidation zones in your chart so you can determine the range the price is moving in.

- Draw trend lines on the chart so that they are more visible. Look for a minimum of two contacts with the trend line.

- Avoid this range and wait, hold your position until you see if the breakout is successful or not. If it fails, it is a fakeout.

- If it is a fakeout, open behind the breakout but in the opposite direction. If the closing price still falls outside of the range, hold your position. It could turn out to be a successful breakout.

- Look for range support for the price target when making short trades. Look for range resistance if you're planning on making long trades.

- Make sure you place your stops above or below the fake candle to prevent major losses.

- Aim for a 1:2 ratio. For example, if the distance to the stop is 50 pips, your target price should be twice that.

Identifying Patterns

Fakeouts can appear in a variety of patterns and can be found in all kinds of market situations. You can usually spot them on technical chart points because those that create them are well aware of the number of investors looking for those points to establish entry positions. As a trader, you need to be able to spot these quickly to avoid getting caught in the trap. If you are smart and can make good decisions, you can do quite well if you follow the pattern of those sharks and reap some of their spoils in the process.

Flags

Technical analysts prefer to create this pattern with two trend lines, keeping the small consolidation period contained in a narrow channel. The normal reaction is to expect the trend to move upwards, which would happen at the break of an upper channel line giving traders the buy signal to start another wave upward.

But with a fakeout, the opposite will happen first, triggering a sell signal. This will cause a slip in the price rather than an increase trapping those who were following the trend just a little too closely.

The smart trader will come in at a very low price and create a better risk-reward ratio, by monitoring this development more closely a nice windfall will be created for him or her.

Triangles

Triangles are another pattern you might observe a fakeout in. Normally, triangles are part of a continuation pattern where the analyst expects a breakout in the same direction as the trend. With a triangle fakeout, a swing trader could take a short position.

Market participants would expect the triangle to be a continuation of the trend and that it would resolve downward. They would assume that there was a start of an upward breakout, which would be a mistake. You will be able to identify this trick the moment the price appears to move in the wrong direction.

Channels

Channels are another way to create a fakeout on the charts. After the analyst has identified a trend he will look for a parallel trend line and connect the highs. Traders will naturally place their stops above the upper line if they plan to trade short or below the support line if they plan to trade long. Top traders are already aware of this move and will place larger orders that will perform in the opposite direction of the intended trend. If they can get over the top, they push the prices upward and will keep pushing until their short orders are executed, thus creating a flood of sell orders. This will force the price back down and back into the channel. The best traders should recognize this move and follow suit, adding to the trend.

As a trader, make sure you wait for the actual fakeout before you get in. It's a good idea to wait until the stops have all been fished out before you enter your position in the channel. This will give you a stronger confirmation as long as you trade in the same direction of the fakeout.

Chapter 5: Momentum Trading

Momentum traders look for acceleration at a stock's price before they enter the market. Once they have identified the momentum, they will take their entry positions with the expectation that the momentum is going to continue to follow that trend. Their method of trade is very similar to those who trade trend channels, but momentum traders are more likely to base their decision on short-term movements rather than on the fundamentals. This type of trading is not always easy and for that reason is more likely to be practiced by more experienced traders.

Timing is a key factor when you're momentum trading. Traders will set their entry points based on the speed of the stock movements and for that reason are much more interested in what's happening in the news at any given point in time. They look for those stocks that are moving to high volumes in reaction to such reports.

To be a momentum trader you have to have a keen sense of concentration and have the ability to stick with it until the target has been reached. Those who are not disciplined enough will usually lose out in this type of trade. The moves often happen very quickly, and their timing has to be absolutely spot-on.

Screening Stocks for Momentum Trading

When looking for potential trades your focus should be placed on the search for trends. Once you find the trends, look to see if there is a strong movement in a specific direction. These movements must be accompanied by a high volume and have lasted over an extended period of time. There are several ways to find these types of trends.

Some traders look at daily watch lists or are continuously monitoring news reports, message boards, or brokerage apps for the latest news that will trigger a high-volume trend.

They will look at stock volume as well. Since their interest lies in the momentum of a trade, the volume will be a major factor to consider. If they notice more buyers than sellers in the market, the price will rise, and more trades will happen.

They will look closely at resistance levels. After they identify the stock trend and its direction, they will search out stocks that are already testing their
46

resistance levels. If they find one that breaks the resistance it is considered a good candidate for momentum trading.

Technical indicators can also help to identify a break in resistance. Momentum traders are more concerned with moves based on a price trend if the stock has passed its point of resistance rather than the traditional buy at the bottom and sell at the top strategy. Once they enter they will stay in the trade until they have reached their target profit amount or hit their stop-loss point.

Short Squeeze

A well-played short squeeze can give an investor quite a bit of profit. Investors look for heavily shorted stocks, so they can maximize their potential for gains.

A short squeeze happens when a stock has a high proportion of short interest as opposed to the overall float. When the value of a stock that is heavily shorted begins to increase, anyone who is trading short starts to lose a substantial amount of money. To cover his position, the investor will have to buy shares in the marketplace. Normally, this action won't have an impact on the price unless there is an excessive amount of short interest in the stock. When that happens, the stocks become flooded with too many of these purchases. The knee-jerk reaction of most traders is their stop-loss positions. These investors will switch positions to become long, pushing the stock price even further along forcing more short positions to close.

Another great way to identify a potential short squeeze is by looking for opportunities to play one. These can be seen when there is a large short percentage of float. One of the best places to look for these is on the NASDAQ. The higher the interest in the 'short' the greater the potential.

You can also check the daily volume. Once you are pretty sure that you know the number of shares being traded on an average day, look for some of the benchmarks that indicate an above average volume of movement in the stock. Take the short interest and divide it by the average daily volume. When there is a higher value for the number of days it is usually an indication that it is a longer squeeze in play.

When you are ready to trade in, ensure that the price is on an upward trend with a bullish push behind it. When everything falls into place, and you are in a long position, ride the wave looking for signs of a pullback.

In this type of trade, it is important to watch the chart closely. Look for the same trends you found when you identified the squeeze but moving in the opposite direction. The volume will begin to spike as the price runs up after people begin to vacate their short positions. This would be a perfect example of watching a short squeeze as it plays out.

Conclusion

Thank you for making it through to the end of *'Swing Trading Strategies: Learn How to Profit Fast with These 4 Simple Strategies,'* let's hope it was informative and able to provide you with all of the tools you need to achieve your goals whatever it may be.

There are many ways one can invest in the stock market, but swing trading seems to be one of the most popular. It doesn't have all the stress of the day trader and you have the ability to take your time as you navigate the market. This could be a very valuable tool when it comes to learning how to trade on the stock market.

The good news is that while in this book, we spent the majority of our time focusing on stocks, the techniques and strategies included here can easily be used in other areas as well. So, whether you prefer to invest in the Forex, currencies, or even cryptocurrencies, the charts, and graphs referred to can all be analyzed in a very similar way.

Even though this book is contained in a very small package there is a lot of information here. It is not likely you will remember it all in one passing so keep it near you as you begin to navigate the market and use it as a reference from time to time. You can also enhance your learning by doing additional research on reputable sites online. No one knows everything there is to know about trading so if you decide to pursue this course of action, remember that you will always be a student.

Still, with the right attitude and diligent application of these strategies, you'll find you will enter the market with a little more confidence than before. As you start, make sure that you start with small trades first, and build up from there. With each success, I'm sure you'll be eager to try more and more, but remember to exercise patience and don't go too deep in the waters until you're sure you can actually pull yourself back to shore when you need to just in case.

Always remember that stock trading is, by its nature, a highly risky venture where you are always in jeopardy of losing everything you put into it. Take your time and be sure about every move you make. Never enter the market without at least two ways to get out of it. Remember to leave your emotions at the door and simply follow the numbers, graphs, and charts and you'll end up trading with nerves of steel that will carry you a long way as a trader who practices swing trading.

Finally, if you found this book useful in any way, a review on Amazon is always appreciated!

Swing Trading Strategies:

Learn How to Profit Fast — Volume 2

Additionally, the information in the following pages is intended only for informational purposes and should thus be thought of as universal. As befitting its nature, it is presented without assurance regarding its prolonged validity or interim quality. Trademarks are mentioned without written consent and can in no way be considered an endorsement from the trademark holder.

Table of Contents

Benefits of undertaking fundamental analysis

Long-term trends

Identify companies with good value

Business acumen

Chapter 4: Basics of Financial Statements

Understanding financial statements
A closer look at financial statements

The balance sheet

Cash flow statement

Basics of financial statements

The income statement

GAAP – Generally Accepted Accounting Principles

Chapter 5: Screening for Undervalued Stocks

Understand why some securities are undervalued

Market corrections and crashes

Cyclic fluctuations

Bad news

Missed expectations

Basic stock screening process
Learn the related terminology

P/E or Price to Earnings ratio

Price-to-Earnings to Growth or PEG

Return On Equity or ROE

Indicators of undervalued stocks

Lagging relative price performance

High dividend yield

1. Determine the indices you wish to compare
2. Note that there are other smaller indices
3. Choose your preferred time frame
4. Check out charting sites and compare prices

Introduction

Congratulations on downloading this book and thank you for doing so.

The following chapters will discuss a number of crucial swing trade strategies that will surely turn you into a pro swing trader. If you want to improve your trading skills and enhance your knowledge about swing trading, then you should read about the great strategies described in this book.

We will focus on proven strategies that will help you succeed in each stage. For instance, the book will teach you how to enter the markets, where to place your stop loss points, and the best exit points. Proper application of these strategies will ensure that you'll trade without being stressed and most of your trades would surely be successful. This way, you will make more money and enjoy trading in the markets.

There are plenty of books on this subject on the market, so thanks again for choosing this one! Every effort was made to ensure that the book is full of as much useful information as possible, please enjoy!

Chapter 1: Basic Swing Trading Strategies

An introduction to swing trading

Swing trading can be described as a type of stock trade where a trader seeks to hold a position in the markets for a period of time longer than one day. The most common period is between 3 to 10 days. However, sometimes the typical plan can last between 1 and 5 days. In rare cases, a position can be held for an entire month.

In swing trading, traders focus on benefiting from a short-term price movement with a large range. This is why, in reality, the definition of swing trading is actually a continuum between day trading and trend trading. A day trader ordinarily holds a position for a brief period of time ranging from a couple of minutes to a couple of hours but never more than an entire day.

On the other hand, a trend trader can hold the stock for a couple of weeks and sometimes, even an entire month. Therefore, a swing trader is simply a trader who holds stocks for a period of time ranging from a few days to a couple of weeks.

Swing trading capitalizes on taking smaller profits within short trends and cutting losses fast. While the gains may be small, they tend to grow very fast over time and can deliver excellent returns at the end of the year.

Essentials of swing trading

As a trader, you need to learn all about the essentials of swing trading. For instance, you need to learn how to determine the best stock to pick. For swing traders, you need to trade in 'large-cap' stocks. Large-cap is a shortened term that means large market capitalization. It refers to stocks with a market capitalization worth at least $10 billion. Stocks are generally labeled as small-cap, mid-cap, or large-cap.

You also need the right market conditions to succeed at swing trading. The market can have two extremes: these are the bull market and the bear market. In such market situations, momentum carries stocks in one direction for lengthy periods of time. So, for swing trading, the best approach is to trade along the long-term trend. It is also crucial to determine the kind of market you will be operating in.

A swing trader will benefit when the markets are headed nowhere. This is when indices rise for a few days, then descend for a couple of days only for the pattern to recur over and over. The swing trader will have plenty of chances to benefit from the short-term 'up and down' movements.

Dow theory and swing trading

The Dow theory implies that the market has always exhibits three distinct trends at the same time. These are the long-term trend, the intermediate trend, and the short-term trends. The short-term trends are also known as the 'day-to-day fluctuations.' Swing traders thrive in the intermediate trend.

- **Long-term trend**
  The long-term trend is mostly used to determine the direction of the trend.

- **Intermediate trend**
  This trend confirms the direction as observed by the long-term trend

- **Short-term trend**

  This particular trend provides price action that can be used to plan out trade entries and exits

Any well-planned swing trading plan should have this structure. However, you will also require technical analysis. This is usually done to confirm or indicate points such as entry, exit, and stop loss.

Swing trading strategy

One of the basics of swing trading strategy is to take modest profits of about 10% rather than 20% to 25%. As a swing trader, your focus is not really in making gains over weeks and months. Most trades last between 5 and 10 days. You will be better off making 5% to 10% gains each week than 20% over a month.

Entry strategy

According to seasoned traders, your swing trading entry strategy is probably the most significant part of your trade. This is because all of your capital will be exposed to risk. However, should the stock finally move in your favor, then you should relax and plan how to collect your profits.

Price pattern

One of the most important aspects of technical analysis used to determine entry points is the 'price pattern.' The price pattern refers to the configuration of price movement. This configuration is identified by using trendlines and curves. There are a couple of price pattern signals that come into play.

A price pattern, can point to a change in trend direction. When this happens, then it is referred to as a 'reversal pattern.' Alternatively, you can have what is known as a 'continuation pattern.' This happens when the current trend proceeds in its intended direction after a brief pause.

Swing points

Identifying swing points should be one of your main intentions with the entry strategy. A swing point is simply a pattern that exhibits three distinct candle patterns. Price patterns have been used by swing traders for many decades. The patterns are the results of the technical analysis.

A trader carries out a technical analysis using price patterns in order to learn more about current market movements and gain insights into future market movements. When it comes to the entry strategy, your first step is to identify any swing points.

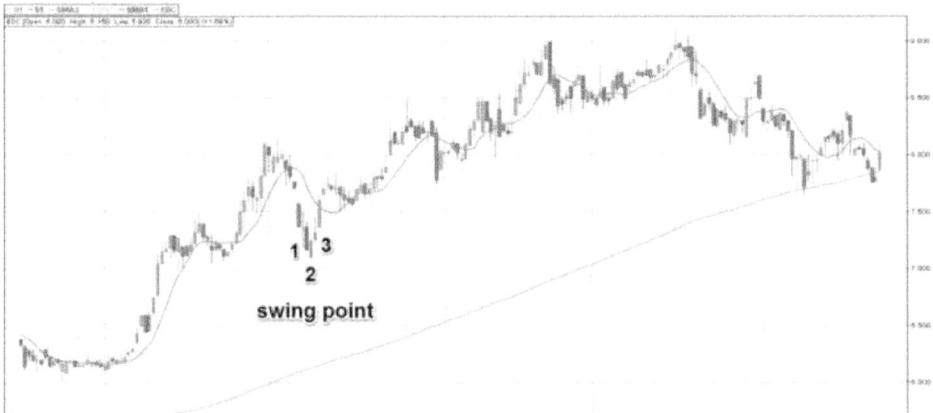

Entry point example

In the example above, our pattern has:

- A low point (1)
- A lower low point (2)
- A higher low point (3)

This is a definite swing point low. In this example, you want to enter the trade at the third candle. Be careful because a reversal always occurs at swing points.

Using swing points to identify reversals

Part of technical analysis performed by traders involves reading charts. When traders keenly observe the technical charting of a stock's price, they are able to identify the moment when a reversal is occurring. Traders usually anticipate a reversal to happen, especially after a stock has been regularly hitting new lows or highs. In these instances, the candlestick movements of the stock are closely observed.

Swing point lows

- The initial candle on the chart makes a low
- The second candle shows a lower low
- The third candle, then results in a higher low

The information derived from the third candle indicates that sellers are rather weak and the stock is very likely to see a price reversal. To be successful in getting a good entry strategy, we need to identify stocks that have both pulled back as they indicate a 'swing point low.' Therefore, our entry strategy in this instance is to identify a stock with a low, a lower low, and then a higher low. At the point of the third candle would be a perfect entry point.

It is crucial to observe that swing points are highly likely to result in a very powerful reversal. This means that if a stock is trending downwards and a swing point occurs, then the price will stop trending downwards and will develop a strong upward trend. This is a great point to enter a trade. However, please also note that reversals do not occur without a swing point developing. You can take the time and look at previous stock charts.

Consecutive price patterns

It is always a great idea to trade stocks with consecutive down days just before the swing point low develops. This is also considered as a great entry point. When you look at your chart, you need to search for consecutive days with an upward trend prior to the appearance of the swing point high.

As you await the development of swing points, you need to watch the left-hand side of the chart to confirm whether your stock is at the resistance or support area of the chart. This is intended to make the strategy more reliable.

Stop loss points

Traders are sometimes wrong and will lose some trades. This is because trading is more of a game of probability. Stop loss points are used to prevent a trader from incurring huge losses and possibly losing large amounts of money.

It is crucial that you make use of stop orders. All too often, enthusiastic traders will take profits quickly, but then lose focus and cling on to losing trades. This is just us being human and is absolutely understandable. However, as a trader, you need to completely detach emotions from your trades. Instead, you need to apply your technical analysis and stick to it.

A well-placed stop order is great because it acts as an insurance against possible huge losses. The stop order works by simply stopping trades once a certain price is attained. When the stop loss order is triggered, it will close out a trade instantly. The order will basically minimize any possible loss. While no trader enters a trade thinking they will lose, losses are part and parcel of a trader's life. However, they really have to be kept in check.

Position size

By setting up a stop loss, you also determine what is referred to as a 'position size.' A position size refers to the size of shares of a stock that you are willing to take. This position is often determined by a simple formula. This formula is used to help minimize your risks while maximizing profitability.

Most traders will not risk losing more than 1% of their total trading capital on one trade. This means that if you have $10,000, then you cannot risk more than $100 on a single trade. However, you need to work out your position size and determine your stop loss then you will be able to assess how you will invest or trade with the $100.

Stop loss and Position size

Let us demonstrate the application of a stop loss with position size. Assume that you have about $15,000 in your trading account. If you set your risks to 1%, it means you will put up to $150 per trade. Now, before you proceed to place a trade on the market, you have to define your stop loss first. Then, you will need to calculate your position size so that you can determine how the $100 will be used.

Now according to your plan, you decide to purchase 100 shares of stock X at the cost of $50. You decide to place a stop loss at $49 which means you are only willing to risk $1 per share. Let us assume that during the trade, the stop loss point is hit. In this case, you risk losing $100. Based on this analysis, you have determined the risk management level to be at 100 shares.

Note that in this case, we are investing a total of $5000 by buying 100 shares at $50 each. However, we stand to lose only $100 if our initial analysis of this particular stock is wrong. Therefore, make sure that you do not arbitrarily place stop loss points. Instead, you should use the price level to determine

68

where they ought to be placed. There are different ways of arriving at the ideal stop loss point. However, one of the most preferred methods is the fixed stop loss.

Fixed stop loss

The fixed stop-loss method is one of the preferred stop loss methods because of its accuracy and reliability. Using the fixed stop-loss method will help you place your stop loss very close to your entry price, but also far enough that it remains untouched if your initial analysis was done incorrectly.

In swing trading, the default stop loss is usually placed at around $0.05 below the prevailing price. This works for many different stocks, especially those within the $5 to $20 range.

Stop loss management

As a beginner, you need to learn about managing your trades and about discipline. Generally, once you determine your stop loss, you need to stick with it. This is also referred to as, "Set it and forget it." When you start adjusting your stop loss points, you complicate matters and allow emotions to lead you. Most new traders do not have the skills or experience to manage their emotions. Therefore, learn some basic stop loss management, such as reducing risks so that your trades are safe and your emotions stable.

Some of the key lessons you need to learn about stop-loss management include:

- Never move a stop loss to manage a growing loss
- Only move a stop loss to lock on profits or to reduce risks

You are highly likely to make most of your trades within the initial stop loss that you determined with your initial analysis. That is if you did your analysis well. You need to note that with swing trading, you should exit when the prevailing share price is close to your stop loss, especially when a major news event is about to be announced.

The stop-loss point can be moved closer to the breakeven point as soon as your trades are 50% trending towards the set target. It can be moved even further once the 75% target is hit. This will guarantee you a profit at this point, no matter what happens.

A trailing stop loss can be initiated when necessary. This is a stop loss that is adjusted as the price adjusts favorably. If you keep winning, then you can move your stop loss in order to lock in profits. Also, if you happen to be watching a trade and the price gets close to the target price, but doesn't seem to get there, then you can exit that trade. Remember, every time that you trade always use a stop loss. This is a trade management tool that you should apply to protect yourself and your capital.

You can use the stop loss to determine other parameters such as your position size. You also need to ensure that you place the stop loss as close to your entry point as possible. This point, however, should not be triggered when the initial trade analysis is correct. This means that the analysis contemplated some movement in the opposite direction, but not too large as to close out the trade. In such instances, you really should let your price get to the stop loss without changing it.

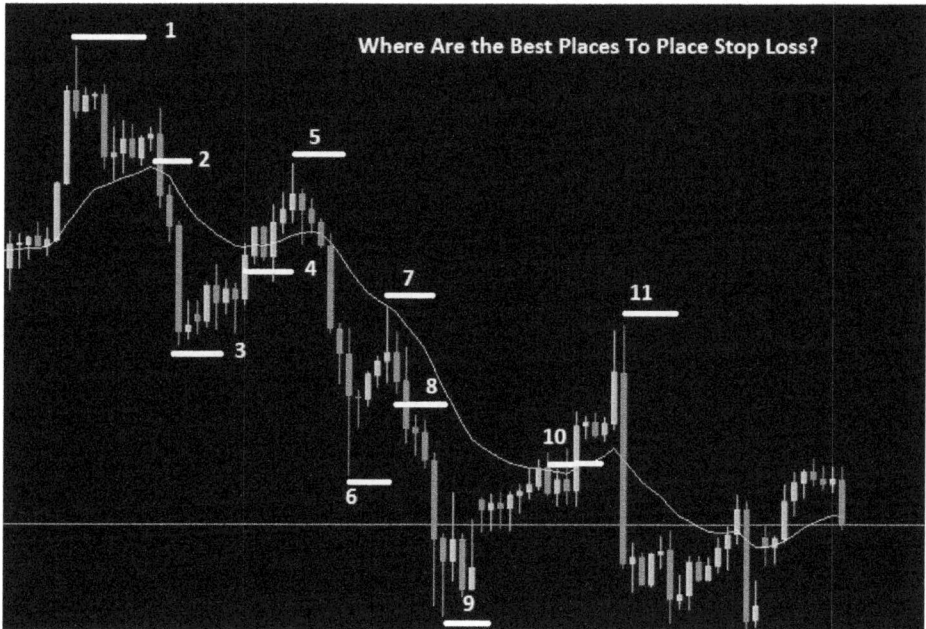

Stop loss Points

EMA – Exponential Moving Average

As a swing trader, one of the most crucial aspects of your technical indicators that you will need is the exponential moving average. The EMA is basically a variation of the SMA (Simple Moving Average), but it places more emphasis on the latest data points. If you use this indicator wisely, then you will be able to identify the entry and exit points and also the trend signals.

The EMA helps you identify the best entry point into any trade. If you observe most charts, you will note that on almost all days the 3-day EMA is featured. For instance, the SPY ETF of December 2015 shows that for three straight months, the daily price was in contact with the 3-day EMA at least 55 times. It only failed to do so 8 times. Therefore, the next time you trade in the market, do not guess the entry or exit points. Instead, use the 3-day

EMA, and either match the price or set it just above or below, depending on the market conditions and how fast you wish to exit a particular trade.

How does the EMA work?

The EMA appears as a line that runs across the price chart. This average uses a mathematical formula to level out the price action. What it does is simply showing the average price of a stock is over a specific period of time. The EMA formula focuses more on recent stock price which makes it much more reliable because it responds faster to the latest price changes.

The important function that this indicator attempts to do is eliminate the confusion regarding the daily price action. The EMA also smooths out the price and reveals any trends. Sometimes, it also reveals some patterns that you would not have seen. The formula is considering more accurate and reliable in predicting future price changes. Here is how the formula looks for a 20-day EMA:

Simple Moving Average (SMA) = [20 – period sum] / 20

The result of this formula reveals the simple moving average. Now we need the multiplier to place more emphasis on the most recent price:

Multiplier = [2/(time period + 1)] = [2/(20+1) = 9.52%

Now we simply need to use these values together to compute the EMA:

*EMA = [Close – (previous day EMA)] * Multiplier + (previous day EMA)*

The accepted protocol is that when the price trades above the EMA, then there is an upward trend and higher prices are to be expected as long as you stay above the EMA. However, when trading below the EMA, then you are experiencing a downward trend, and you can expect lower prices as long as you stay beneath the EMA.

Trading the 3-day EMA can be very profitable for traders. You can easily net in close to $100, for instance, if you close a trade at 208 rather than 207. This additional income, repeated week after week, will add up to a satisfying amount by the year's end. Also, trading this particular indicator will protect you from the high volatility exhibited by some high beta stocks.

You should consider using the short EMA on weekly charts in order to manage trades that have longer holding periods. Whichever way you use it, the EMA approach is one that you want to use regularly as a swing trader.

Chapter 2: Swing Trading Tools and Resources

To be a successful trader, you will need access to reliable resources. The good news is that there are plenty of excellent resources all across the web. These resources include educational materials, online brokers, real-time securities market data, and super-fast computer networks.

Sometimes, you may not have access to all the resources necessary, and you may have to choose between what is essential and what you can afford. A little research goes a long way in helping you make crucial decisions about your trades. It is advisable to know more about the kind of resources available to you. These resources are ideal for swing traders.

Software for technical analysis

A key part of your life as a trader will involve the use of charts. In fact, there are people who believe swing traders are only as productive as their charting software. You will spend a good amount of time reading charts and interpreting data on screens. Electronic trading platforms and market software are crucial resources of any serious trader.

You can get most of the trading software from your preferred broker. There are other types of software programs available from software vendors. The trading software comes with a wide variety of functions including analysis functions, stock screening, research, and even trade. In fact, trading software comes with built-in integrated additions like technical indicators, alert features, news, trade automation, fundamental analysis numbers, and much more.

The Worden TC2000

This is a powerful trading software that is exclusive to the US and Canadian markets. With this software, you can expect to get different watch lists, stock charts, news, sorting, scanning, and messaging. You will get access to over 70 technical indicators, fundamental data coverage, and an easy-to-use interface that makes trading a breeze, as well as over 70 technical indicators as along with 10 drawing tools. Some tools are not available, however, like automated trading tools. You will also be limited to trading ETFs, funds, and stocks.

MetaStock

Another widely used stock trading software, this software comes packed with over 300 technical indicators. It also comes with other useful tools such as the Fibonacci retracement tool, global market data, and fundamental data complete with filtering and screening options, as well as integrated news. Some of the assets that are accessible include commodities, futures, forex, equities, and derivatives. Its two packages, MetaStock Real-Time and MetaStock Daily Charts come with the superbly useful stock charts software.

NinjaTrader

This is a popular integrated charting and trading software system. It is a highly-regarded software mostly because it provides end-to-end solutions from the time you enter a trade until you exit. Ninja Trader comes with third-party library integration and customizable, reliable development options. It is perfect for both trade and research. It is not a free platform to use, but it's pretty affordable. Some of its immensely useful features include research, fundamentals, and charting tools along with over 100 technical indicators. It also provides a modern trade simulator. This way, you can trade without risks and learn crucial tips and lessons.

VectorVest

If you wish to trade across markets in different countries, then this is the best platform for you. The VectorVest is an amazing trading platform that comes with analytics software that covers varied regions. These include Singapore, India, Hong Kong, South Africa, Canada, UK, and the USA. It is, therefore, suitable for the international trader, especially those who prefer trading across major funds and stock markets across the world. Other features include stock watchlists, real-time filtering, customization, back-testing capabilities, and charting lists.

Other useful or notable software analysis programs include Trade Trakker, TradeSpoon, Market Club, and TradeMiner. Tradespoon come with an algorithm that is capable of accurately predicting future prices. Trade Trakker is very easy to use and is suitable for trading and keeping track of your trading activity.

Trading and data

As a trader, you will be making most of your decisions based on data. Which is why you need to have access to reliable data such as stock prices and so on. Long-term investors do not necessarily worry about accurate stock prices in the short term. However, for swing traders, it is essential to have access to the latest trading data.

The good news is that most online brokers provide traders with some form of data. All this data is mostly free. The platforms consistently receive data streams throughout. This data is crucial for most traders. Sometimes real-time data is not free, and as a trader, you will have to determine which data you need and which you will pay for. Always ensure that you have access to all the data you require during trading.

Swing trade charts

Swing trade charts are of paramount importance for your technical analysis. They are crucial for a couple of reasons. Here are some of these reasons:

- These charts show market trends. Trends are the primary means of profiting in any market

- They portray very little unnecessary data which is great as it improves the accuracy of your technical analysis

- There are different variations of swing charting that can enhance the prospects of identifying market trends

How to use swing charts

Swing charts enable you to view the overall trend of the market or even a specific stock. You can tell the trend by searching for 'progressive higher' as well as 'higher lows.' These usually produce a pattern similar to a staircase. You can also discern market trends by drawing trend lines.

They make it easier to apply technical analysis techniques, especially those not affected by time. Some of these include Elliott waves and Fibonacci levels. By doing these calculations, you will learn where the price is headed and also determine better stop-loss and take-profit points.

You can use the results of your analysis to determine price channels. You can do this by simply connecting consecutive highs together with consecutive lows. Price channels that you develop will help you predict prices, determine stop-loss, and take-profit points. It will also assist you in adding or liquidating a position in good time. Price usually moves through the lines that connect low to lows and highs to highs.

This is why it's crucial to make use of swing charts as they provide a simple method of viewing trends. The charts remove both time factor as well as market noise. You can use other additional tools just to confirm what the charts already indicated. Always remember, as a trader, that the trend is your friend and swing charts will enable you to identify the trend.

Use oscillators and candlestick charts

As a swing trader, you need to learn how to use different technical analysis tools. These will help make your trades more successful by helping you take advantage of short-term price movements. To determine both the trend strength and direction, you will probably have to use fractals, oscillators, volume analysis, chart patterns, and other methods.

Some of the most crucial methods that you should master are candlestick and oscillator patterns. These patterns provide an easy and quick method that characterizes the trend in order to identify swing trends. Here is a look at some of these methods:

Divergence and Convergence

The term divergence and convergence refer to the moments when the price movement of a stock differs significantly from that of the moment indicators. This method compares to throwing a ball up in the air. After a while, the ball will lose momentum before it starts to fall down. This is the exact same thing that happens to stock prices as momentum first slows down just before the stock price changes direction. Convergence, together with divergence, will indicate when the momentum is pulling back, and a possible reversal may occur.

Indecision candles

Traders use candlestick charts regularly because they are designed to assist them in accurately interpreting the price movement of a stock. Generally, the candle's body represents the closing and opening, whereas the tails on the candle's ends indicate the price movements of the day. We can, therefore, characterize indecision as a situation where we have volatility but without any movement. Such a situation is also referred to as 'long tails and a short body.' These candles are usually observed just before a trend changes direction.

How to clearly point out a reversal

At this stage, you want to clearly point out or accurately define the point of reversal. This needs to be as close to perfection as possible. There are close to 60 candlestick patterns, but only a couple can indicate consistent and reliable reversal points.

Bullish and Bearish engulfing

Among the most crucial candlestick patterns are the bullish and bearish engulfing. The reason why they are so important is that they are extremely reliable. For our purposes, we need to pay close attention to the lengths of the candlesticks. Basically, the initial candlestick needs to be shorter on low volume followed by the next which should be long with high volume. When this situation occurs, then it points to indecision, which marks the last stages of a trend before a reversal actually takes place.

The Harami Cross

Yet another superbly common and useful candlestick reversal pattern is the 'Harami Cross.' With this pattern, you need to keep a close eye on volumes. You should look out for volume buildup as the trend heads upwards and towards the cross. The volume is expected to decrease, and short tails will form on the Harami Cross candle. The reduction in volume and formation of short tails is a clear indication that traders have lost confidence in the stock and a reversal should occur at any time.

As a trader, you need to learn how to use oscillators and candlesticks. These will give you an easy and speedy way of identifying swing trades. You can add these techniques with others like volume analysis, fractals, and chart patterns. This way, you will increase your accuracy and your trades will be profitable.

Other swing trade resources
Screeners

As a trader, you need to determine the particular stocks you will trade in. for this, you will need to use screeners. A screener is simply a filtering tool that helps you identify stocks that you can trade in. You need to ensure that you find a screener that can filter out all the parameters you desire. A filtering criterion should be prepared beforehand.

For instance, if you have a trading strategy that incorporates the 150-day moving average, but your screening tool does not have this provision, then you should try and find another one. Screeners help you to zero in on a particular stock if you have hundreds of potential stocks.

A watchlist

One of the best ways of tracking potential future trades is by creating and maintaining a watchlist. This is easy to do online because there are plenty of trading sites that offer this service. It is even possible to integrate the service with a trading platform. You do not have to pay for this service because it is essentially just a list of stocks. You can easily find software that you can use to create your own list. Once you have prepared your own list, you can then organize it and manage it any way you want. You can even come up with a sub-list. As a rule, you should maintain a list and try and ensure it is independent of any websites. This is because sites that do offer a service charge for providing that kind of information are sometimes unavailable.

Backtesters

Historical market data is normally used by back testers to test a trading strategy. These are often websites designed for this very purpose. Some are more sophisticated, but most are limited in their functionality depending on the criteria.

At other times, testing is restricted to a given data set. On the other hand, the more sophisticated backtesters will allow you to define your own data set and even draft your own script. A lot of traders skip this step, but if you have a complex swing trading strategy, then it is advisable to use the backtest to confirm that it will work as desired.

Chapter 3: Fundamental Analysis of Company Stock

What is a fundamental analysis?

When it comes to trading, fundamental analysis can be described as a method of evaluating securities such as stocks. The aim is to measure the intrinsic value of a company or its stock. We carry out a fundamental analysis by closely examining financial reports, economic prospects, as well as other quantitative and qualitative factors. Basically, you study anything that pertains to the value of the company's security.

Fundamental analysts often study anything that can affect a security. These include both macroeconomic and microeconomic factors that touch on securities. Macroeconomic factors include specific industry conditions and anything that has an effect on the economy.

There are plenty of professionals who conduct stock and company analysis. They include traders such as stock traders, stock analysts, fund managers, and many others. As a swing trader, you need to learn how to carry out a thorough fundamental analysis of any stock or security that you are interested in. Fundamental analysis is the backbone of any investment process. You can only be regarded as a successful trader or investor if you can successfully perform fundamental analysis.

Basics of fundamental analysis

Fundamental analysis is often conducted to determine the performance and health of the underlying company. This is often achieved by examining certain economic indicators and key figures. Doing so provides information that helps us identify successful companies and industries as well as those that are fundamentally weak. This allows investors to go short on weak companies and long on companies with strong fundamentals. This type of analysis where we look closely at a company's fundamentals is often considered as the opposite of technical analysis.

For a successful evaluation of a company's fundamentals, you have to delve deep into their financial statements. This process is also known as 'quantitative analysis' where you will examine the assets and liabilities of a company, expenses, revenue, and all other aspects related to the company's finances. In doing your fundamental analysis, you have to examine all this information so that you get a good look at a company's future performance. Learning about cash flow statements, income statements, and balance sheets are also a crucial part of fundamental analysis.

However, apart from quantitative analysis, you will also be required to perform some qualitative analysis when performing fundamental analysis. While this method is largely used to evaluate stocks, it can also be used to analyze any other type of security.

Take the example of an investor looking to invest in bonds. This investor can make a fundamental analysis to determine the bond's actual value while examining certain economic factors like interest rates and the general state of the national economy. Other information that is relevant is the company's ratings with credit firms. When it comes to equities and stocks, fundamental analysis takes into consideration factors such as future growth, earnings, profit margins, return on equity, revenue, and other data in order to determine the firm's underlying value as well as its potential for further growth in future.

Fundamental analysis example

One of the world's best known and most successful stock analysts is Mr. Warren Buffett. He uses fundamental analysis to determine which shares to buy and which companies to invest in. His success as an analyst has turned him into a billionaire.

Apart from analyzing companies, the equities market can also be analyzed. There are some analysts who conducted a fundamental analysis on the S&P 500 for a period of less than one week. This was from 4th July to 8th July 2016. Within this period of time, the S&P index went up to 2129.90 following the release of an impressive jobs report within the US. This was an unprecedented performance surpassed only by May 2015 which was 2132.80. The superb performance was attributed to the announcement of 287,000 new jobs across the country.

What does 'fundamental' refer to?

When we talk about fundamentals, we actually mean the quantitative and qualitative data that significantly contribute to the success and financial valuation of a company. It also includes assessment of both macroeconomics and microeconomics. These are aspects that are essential for determining the worth of a company or other assets.

Microeconomics and Macroeconomics

Macroeconomics stands for all factors that affect the general economy. These are factors such as inflation, supply and demand, unemployment, and even

GDP growth. They also include international trade and prevailing monetary and fiscal policies put forth by the authorities. Macroeconomic considerations are useful when it comes to matters of large-scale analysis of the economy and how these relate to business activities.

Microeconomic factors are those that focus on the smaller elements of the economy. These include elements in certain particular sectors of a market. For example, labor issues in a given market, matters such as supply and demand, and others, such as labor and consumer issues relating to the said industry.

Stock analysis

Stock analysis can be defined as the process used by traders and investors to acquire in-depth information about a stock or company. The analysis is done by evaluating and studying current and past data about the stock or even the company itself. This way, traders, and investors can gain a significant edge in the market as they will be in a position to make well-informed decisions.

Technical analysis versus Fundamental analysis

When analyzing a stock, analysts usually perform both fundamental and technical analysis. Fundamental analysis relies mostly on different sources of data, such as economic reports, financial records, market share, and company assets. For publicly listed companies, the data are usually sourced from financial statements such as cash flow statements, income statements, footnotes, and balance sheets.

Such information is readily available to the public via 10-K and 10-Q reports. You can access the reports via the EDGAR database system that is managed by the SEC or Securities and Exchange Commission. Data can also be sourced from the earnings reports which are often released quarterly.

Fundamental analysis

Some of the parameters that analysts look at within a company's financial statement include a measure of solvency, profitability, liquidity, growth trajectory, efficiency, and leverage. Analysts also use ratios to work out the financial health of companies. Examples of these ratios include quick ratio and current ratio. These rations are useful in determining a company's ability to repay short-term liabilities based on its current assets.

To find the current ratio, you have to divide the current assets with the current liabilities. These figures can easily be accessed from the company's balance sheet. While there is no ratio that is considered ideal, anything below 1 is considered a poor financial situation where a company is incapable of meeting all short-term debts.

The balance sheet also provides analysts with additional information such as current debt amounts owed by the company. In such a situation, then the analysis will focus on the debt ratio. This is computed by working out all the liabilities and dividing it by the total assets. When the ratio is computed, a ratio greater than 1 points to a company with a lot more debt compared to its assets. This means that should interest rates rise, then the firm may default on its debts.

Stock analysis involves not just current financial reports, but also compares the current financial statements with those from previous years. This will give a trader or investor a feel of the company's performance and will determine whether the firm is stable, receding, or growing. It is also common for an analyst to compare a company's financial statement with those of other companies in the same sector. This is done in order to compare profitability and other parameters.

Of great importance is the operating profit. It is a measure of the revenue that a company is left with after other expenses have been cleared. Basically, a firm with operating margins of 0.27 is viewed favorably when compared with one whose margin is 0.027, for instance. This can be translated to mean that the firm whose operating margin is 0.27 spends 73 cents per dollar earned to support its operating costs.

Technical analysis

This is another method used by analysts, investors, and traders to analyze stocks and companies. This type of analysis pays closer attention to previous market action and how this can be used to predict future performance. In this instance, an analyst, or trader, will analyze the entire market and will focus their attention on volume and price. Other factors looked at include supply and demand as well as any essential factors that can move the market.

One of the most crucial tools for technical analysis is a chart. Charts are key for successful analysis of any market, particular stocks, or companies. They provide a graphical presentation of a stock and its trend within a given time period. For instance, a technical analyst can use a chart to indicate which areas are either on resistance or support levels.

Resistance levels are placed above a stock's prevailing market price while support levels are indicated by previous lows that occur just below the current or prevailing market price. Should there be a break below support levels, this points to a bearish trend in the market. On the other hand, any break that occurs just above resistance levels will point to a bullish outlook.

Factors that influence stock prices

Technical analysis outcomes are only effective if the analysis of the price trend is affected by demand and supply forces. However, when other external factors come into play and affect price movement, then a technical analysis of stocks may not be successful. For instance, stock prices can be affected by factors such as dividend announcements, the death of a company CEO, mergers, stock splits, change of management or monetary policy, and so on.

It is common for analysts to conduct both technical and fundamental analysis together, even though they can be conducted separately. Some choose to apply only one while others prefer both methods for stock and company analysis. In order to come up with a successful investment strategy for your portfolio, then you need to do some analysis and assess market sectors, stocks, and the markets themselves.

Procedure for fundamental evaluation

There is generally no clear-cut method provided on how to conduct a fundamental analysis, but there are some generally accepted norms. The best approach is often a top-down method where you begin by examining the overall economy. From there, you will analyze different industries followed by specific companies.

You should keep in mind that the information you acquire is relative. Also, ensure that you compare firms within the same sector. If you are looking at an automobile company like General Motors, then you can only compare it with other companies in the same industry, for instance, Ford Motors.

Overall economic forecast

The first step you need to take is to evaluate the general situation of the overall economy. You can think of the economy as a tide with the different companies and sectors as ships in the sea. Should the economy be in decline, then most of the companies and industries will also be in decline. One of the leading indicators of economic contraction and expansion is the interest rate. They are also a leading indicator of the market's condition.

Industry selection

As the economy expands, there are certain industries that are likely to benefit from it more than others. It is possible for an investor to narrow down their list of industries to those that are likely to benefit from the current state of the economy. A risk in equities' investment is considered low when most companies are likely to benefit from the economy. A growth strategy can be adopted with investments in sectors such as semiconductors, biotech, and technology.

When the economy is contracting, then an investor may wish to be more conservative and buy stocks in industries that are more stable such as energy, utilities, and consumer staples. Factors that you should consider when evaluating companies include market size, overall growth rate, and its ranking in the general economy. It is much more important to be in the right group as stocks often move together with very few lone stocks out there.

Narrow down an industry

As soon as you identify the best industry, the next step is to narrow down the industry to a few companies. The most common approach is to identify the leading firms as well as innovators in a specific industry. Most successful companies often have an edge over the others. It could be their marketing skills, market share, technology, innovation, and so on. Conduct a comparative analysis of the companies in the chosen industry and come up with a short list.

Company analysis

Once you have a short list of firms in a given industry, you should then conduct an analysis of each company especially in regards to their capabilities and resources. The companies selected should have a desirable business plan, a sound financial foundation, and proper management.

If you're looking at the company's business plan, you want to see whether the business is feasible. You also need to know if the company is a market leader and if their direction is clearly defined. These are all crucial factors that you need to examine and consider. Another thing that's important is the company's management. You need to examine the managers and find out about their skills, experience, and talents. Finally, you will also be required to look at the company's financial statements. This is what we will examine in the next chapter.

Benefits of undertaking fundamental analysis

There are lots of benefits of conducting a thorough fundamental analysis of a company. Here is a look at some of these benefits:

Long-term trends

Fundamental analysis is excellent for investors and traders, especially long-term investors. Patient investors who are planning to invest in the long-term as well as traders seeking solid, reliable companies will definitely benefit from doing the analysis.

Identify companies with best value

Reliable fundamental analysis enables investors and traders to identify firms that are of high value and worth investing in. A lot of notable investors always look for valuable companies. They include John Neff and Warren Buffett. Valuable companies will have a strong balance sheet, staying power, stable earnings, and valuable assets.

Business acumen

Fundamental analysis will help you develop a deep understanding of the business. For instance, you will become familiar with profit drivers and revenue sources of the company. For instance, earning expectations and actual earnings are extremely useful when it comes to equity and stock prices.

Chapter 4: Basics of Financial Statements

Understanding financial statements

Financial statements are statements that try to accurately present the financial and operations position of a business. Most established firms work on the framework of 4 distinct financial statements. These statements are:

- Income statement
- Balance sheet
- Statement of changes in equity
- Cash flow statement

It is considered to be standard practice for companies to periodically release financial statements that largely conform to GAAP or 'Generally Accepted Accounting Principles.' This approach helps ensure the continuity of information and data presentation across national and international borders.

Company and business financial statements are generally audited by accountants, government agencies, audit firms, and so on. This ensures the accuracy of reporting for purposes of investing, financing, and even tax matters.

A closer look at financial statements

Traders, investors, and analysts often rely on the latest information and data provided in order to analyze and make informed predictions about the next course of action of a stock price. They use various financial statements from companies. One of the most common of these statements is the company's annual report. This report contains the company's financial statements. These often include a balance sheet, income statement, and a cash flow statement.

The balance sheet

One of the most crucial financial statements of any business is its balance sheet. This statement provides deeper insights into a company's liabilities, assets, and equities. The report is often released at the end of every financial year.

The balance sheet has a simple equation which is that total assets must equal total liabilities plus the stockholder's equity. The reason for this is that assets are often paid for using liabilities like loans and stockholder's equity like additional capital and retained earnings. On this same report, assets are indicated and ranked based on the order of liquidity. The most liquid asset, which is cash, is listed at the top. On the other hand, liabilities are published on the same page in the order in which they will be sorted. Current liabilities like short-term debts are expected to be paid off in a year or less while the non-current liabilities are often paid off over a year or more.

Cashflow statement

This is a financial statement that combines both the income statement and the balance sheet. The cash flow report is meant to reconcile the balance sheet with the income statement in 3 practical ways. These 3 are investing, financing, and operating activities.

Operating activities may include money coming in from general business activities. Financing activities of a company include any incoming funds from equity and debts while investing activities refer to income generated from the purchase and disposal of assets like equipment and real estate.

Basics of financial statements

Basically, the balance sheet informs you if a company or business pays its debts on time. In short, it provides you with an insight into a firm's financial position up to the date of preparation.

- **Assets**

  These are items that have future economic and financial benefits

- **Liabilities**

  These are financial obligations that have to be settled using assets

- **Equity**

It refers to the residual interest of a firm once you deduct the liabilities from assets

The crucial accounting equation of any balance sheet is: $A = L + OE$.
This simply means *Assets = Liabilities + Owners Equity.*

Assets can be broken down further into current and long-term (noncurrent). They are usually listed according to how easily they can be converted into cash.
This is also referred to as 'liquidity.'

Liabilities are often listed according to the expected order in which they will be paid. Current liabilities are those expected to be paid within a year or less. They include deposits, advances, trade notes payable, and accounts payable. Examples of non-current liabilities are long-term debts, mortgages, bonds payable, and so on.

All this information provides analysts and traders with crucial information. For instance, they can discern how risky a firm's financial structure is, how it compares with other companies within the same industry and so on. If the debt is too high, then this can be risky should the company go through tough times and rough patches. If the debt is too low, then probably the company is not expending all its leverage and might be growing at the levels it should. This could give an edge to competitors and weary investors.

The information can also provide an estimate of how liquid a company is. A firm's current assets are assessed against its current liabilities. A liquid company is more flexible and can achieve a lot compared to a company that isn't.

The income statement

The income statement is also referred to as the 'profit and loss statement.' It provides useful insights into the profitability and earnings of a company. This statement is time specific and only showcases the income accrued within a given time such as a quarter or a month.

It is important that the income statement is periodic as it makes comparisons relatively simple. You can compare the income statements of different companies for a specific period of time or consecutive periods. Also, year-over-year comparisons actually eliminate seasonal deficiencies, and this can prove to be substantially useful in some instances.

GAAP – Generally Accepted Accounting Principles

One of the most crucial aspects of financial statements is that they can be compared to others, especially between companies within the same industry. This is the reason why statements of accounts are usually prepared according to the 'Generally Accepted Accounting Principles' or GAAP.

GAAP consists of rules, standards, procedures, and conventions that are crucial in defining generally accepted accounting practices at any given period of time. The current GAAP is the U.S. GAAP which consists of practices from the FASB and other predecessors. As new research is performed and business conditions change, the standards are amended while others are eliminated.

Accounting is simply the way businesses keep a tab on all their financial activities. The data are usually consumed internally and acts as a useful tool for any business. It helps give useful advice if budgets and internal goals are not being achieved. Accounting data are sometimes used by internal factors such as investors and potential creditors. It is important therefore that this data is uniform so that disseminating it is simple.

There are plenty of established accounting standards while others continue to evolve. Only very few are debatable or highly controversial. Accounting standards and practices will continue to improve and evolve with time as businesses grow and expand. There are, for instance, challenges and new opportunities posed by online businesses that have not been addressed by current accounting standards. It is hoped that this will change soon as the rules and standards keep evolving with time.

Chapter 5: Screening for Undervalued Stocks

There are some stocks in the market that are undervalued and others that could be overvalued. Many investors and traders are always on the lookout for undervalued stocks to add to their portfolios. A lot of investors believe that identifying undervalued stocks is one way of finding great investments. This is because these stocks are often priced at levels far below their underlying values. To understand this concept of value investing, we need to go into detail about a few things.

Understand why some securities are undervalued

It is important that you understand as much as possible about value investing. Therefore, you need to learn and understand why some stocks or securities become undervalued. One of the crucial reasons for value investing is because stock markets sometimes undervalue stocks occasionally. There are reasons why this happens so let us have a look at some of these reasons:

- **Market corrections and crashes**
  When the market drops, then investors are provided with an excellent chance to search for a variety of undervalued stocks.

- **Cyclic fluctuations**
  These tend to happen from time to time where some sectors outperform others. This happens in various stages of the regular economic cycle. The sectors that are disadvantaged by the fluctuations often offer excellent sources for undervalued stocks.

- **Bad news**

  Whenever there is bad news, it results in serious knee-jerk reactions that cause stock prices to plummet far more than they should. This is almost similar to stocks not meeting an analyst's expectations.

- **Missed expectations**

  In some instances, quarterly results can fall far short of expectation. This can be a pretty serious issue and can cause shares to plunge a lot more than they should.

Now, if you wish to screen for undervalued stocks and shares, then you should confine your efforts only to businesses that you understand. However, this only applies to investors. Apparently far too many investors, venture into industries that they do not completely understand, and this puts their investments at risk.

You also need to understand the related terminology and metrics essential for stock evaluation. While there are plenty of metrics, there are some important ones that you should learn.

Basic stock screening process

There are a few basic steps that you can follow in order to identify undervalued stocks. You first need to come up with a general list of stocks that you wish to investigate further. These are stocks that qualify after passing the basic screening process and happen to be in industries that you understand. Once you have this basic list, you may then proceed to do a more in-depth research and analysis to actually identify the kind of stock you are looking for. You can search for shares that you like through databases such as SEDAR for Canadian firms and EDGAR for US-based companies.

There are tons of free web-based tools that can assist you in searching and screening for stocks and shares. Think of tools such as Yahoo Stock Screener or Google Stock Screener. These are free and readily accessible. You can get even more detailed results by using paid services from sites like YChart Stock Screener. Screeners generally analyze thousands of stocks and then screen them according to the criteria that you provided. One of the most important search criteria used is P/E. You can set the screeners to only find stocks with P/E lower than 15. Screeners will do just that and only show you companies with P/E lower than 15.

Learn the related terminology

There are plenty of metrics related to stock evaluation. For our purposes, we only need to learn some of them and not all. Here are some metrics that are essential for identifying undervalued stocks:

- **P/E or Price to Earnings ratio**
  One of the most useful metrics used to evaluate stocks is P/E or price to earnings ratio. This ratio is obtained simply by dividing the current stock price to its annual earnings. The result will give a metric that can be used to compare firms within the same industry or sector. Ideally, a lower P/E ratio means the stock is undervalued. And this is just one among many other metrics.

- **Price-to-Earnings to Growth or PEG**

  This is another important ratio used to determine undervalued stocks. You calculate the PEG by dividing the P/E ratio with the projected earnings growth rate within a given period of time. It is crucial to also use this value to compare the performance of a business vis-à-vis the performance of other firms in the same sector.

- **Return On Equity or ROE**

  A return on equity is yet another metric you can use to find undervalued stocks. ROE refers to a firm's annual net income calculated as a percentage of the shareholders' equity. In short, this metric measures the efficiency of a company in investing funds to create wealth.

- **Debt to Equity ratio**

  The debt to equity ratio is a ratio that computed by working out a firm's total debt and dividing this debt with the total shareholders' equity.

- **Current ratio**

  The current ratio is more of a liquidity related metric. It is computed by taking a company's current assets and dividing it by the total of its current liabilities. This ratio informs investors the ease at which a firm repays its short-term debt.

You should begin evaluating stocks in order to get a feel of some of these metrics. You can also develop your very own evaluation criteria to find undervalued stocks in the market.

Let us say you are searching the markets for undervalued stocks, you will do well by searching for ROE that is 15% or better, debt to equity ratio of 0.5 or below, and a below average P/E for stocks in the same industry. These guidelines are not really cast in stone and analysts are allowed to be flexible. Basically, these are just some of the useful guidelines that you will need in your evaluation process.

Indicators of undervalued stocks
Lagging relative price performance
An underperformance of company stock occurs when the company's share price is considerably low in comparison to those of its peers within the industry. There are many reasons why this can happen. One reason is when stock analysts express their concerns because of certain metrics. It is not unlikely that just a single voice on major networks will voice their concerns and send prices tumbling down. Investors tend to follow suit and further drive down the price, causing the stock to be undervalued.

High dividend yield
When a firm's dividend payment rate is much higher than that of competitors, then this could also point to a dip in stock price. This dip could be sufficiently low to indicate undervalued in relation to the dividend payout. However, should the company become stable and other dividend payouts seem secure, then the dividends can seem like a short-term gain. Anyone using screeners should apply the dividend yield percentage to obtain metrics.

Low Price-to-Earnings ratio

One of the most common measures of a stock's relative value is the price to earnings ratio or P/E. While it may not be the best measure of a stock's valuation, it is still a very popular metric. Each company has its own P/E ratio and the higher it is, then the higher the stock price will be compared to the profits. A low P/E ratio is sometimes an indicator of a good buying opportunity. Sometimes, there is a reason behind this. Investors who pay a keen interest in a company can easily know if the company is hiding some information.

A Low Market-to-Book ratio

There are companies with a low market value when compared to the book value or total equity. This is often an undervaluation. The crucial matter here is to understand the actual value of all the tangible assets. These include buildings, land, and cash. You also need to value the intangible assets such as intellectual property, goodwill, and so on.

Take the example of a firm that produces shoes. The company may also own the land on which they operate on, and this land may be worth more than the shoe production facilities. However, this value will not reflect on the analysis or the stock price and will not be reflected in the books.

Free cash flow

A lot of investors and traders focus more on free cash flow and less on reported profit. Free cash flow is basically money that is generated by a firm when all expenses and costs and accounted for. There are stocks that may appear to be lowly-priced simply because of lower reported earnings. Such stocks may represent firms with decent cash flow. It is advisable to use a screener to identify companies through the cash or share ratio.

Analyzing undervalued stocks

Undervalued stocks have been defined as stocks that are priced at 30% or more below their intrinsic value. Therefore, to determine whether a stock is undervalued or not, you will have to work out its intrinsic value. Most people have no idea how to get this value simply because they did not attend business school. Fortunately, it is easy to do so using the software on your computer. If you have spreadsheet software, then you can find out a company's intrinsic value.

Insider purchasing activity

In any company, we have insiders who can affect factors such as stock price, share value, intrinsic value, and so on. An insider within a company is any senior executive such as officers with executive authority and directors who own at least 10% of company shares. These senior company officials have intrinsic knowledge about the company. When they purchase its stock, then you can assume that the company is financially stable and sound. However, when they begin selling off their shares, then you will know that trouble is probably not far off.

The art of value investing

The best way you can successfully invest in undervalued stocks is to conduct thorough research on the company. It is not by looking at a couple of ratios that seem good on the surface. Ratios never tell the whole story, but just provide a guide that you can use together with other tools in your analysis of stocks. You also need to use critical thinking and some common sense during the entire process.

Experts in the field of value investing such as Christopher H. Browne recommend asking a company serious questions. For instance, how are the company's future prospects like? Can the company still be profitable if they increased prices at a future date? Are there any competitors and are they a serious challenger? What are the growth prospects of the company?

Answering these questions, or what you think the answers are, is basically the essence of value investing. Value investing is more of an art form. It requires your intuition, thoughts, queries, and judgment. Simply entering numbers into the software will just not do. When answering these questions, you need to exert effort in increasing your accuracy. To achieve this, you should invest in companies that you understand well or companies whose products you are familiar with.

Let us say you have worked in the biotech or software industry for a couple of years. This means that you are intimately familiar with the particular industry and have a better understanding of the business than the average person. Also, if you are a buyer of household goods, kitchen appliances, cars, or electronics, then you probably know a lot about these industries. As a retail investor, you are actually capable of outperforming other investors by jumping in early before Wall Street catches on.

Simply taking a closer look at stocks will not actually help you much, as you also need to do a lot of critical thinking. You will, for instance, never know when a new invention will make current products or services obsolete. However, it is possible to find out exactly how a company has fared in the field of research and development and how it has adapted to change through the years.

This is why it is sometimes good to also take a closer look at a company's management and its board of directors as well. Firms that have a good track record of adopting changes and reforming their operations are better positioned to adapt should new inventions hit the market. Those with a poor track record of change and research will probably not fare as well when real change or new innovations hit the market.

Chapter 6: Technical Analysis to Determine Entry Points

Technical analysis

As we have already determined, technical analysis is simply the process of forecasting the future movement of stocks on the markets according to past stock price movements. Just like weather predictions, technical analysis has not produce 100% accurate results.

However, technical analysis provides traders and investors with the information they can use to anticipate the price movement over time. There are a wide variety of charts that are used to help determine the future price movements of a particular stock.

Factors related to technical analysis

Technical analysis can be applied to numerous securities, including Forex, stocks, futures, commodities, indices, and many more. The price of a security depends on a collection of metrics. These are volume, low, open, high, close, open interest, and so on. These are also known as market action or price data.

There are a couple of assumptions that we make as traders when performing technical analysis. However, remember that it is applicable only in situations where the price is only a factor of demand and supply. Should there exist other factors that can influence prices significantly, then technical analysis will not work. The following assumptions are often made about securities that are being analyzed.

There are no artificial price movements

Artificial price movements are usually a result of distributions, dividends, and splits. Such changes in stock price can greatly alter the price chart, and this tends to cause technical analysis to be very difficult to implement. Fortunately, it is possible to remedy this. All that you need to do as an analyst is to make adjustments to historical data before the price changes.

The stock is highly liquid

Another major assumption that technical analysis makes is that stocks are highly liquid. Liquidity is absolutely crucial for volumes. When stocks are heavily traded as a result of liquidity and volume, then traders can easily enter and exit trades. Stocks that are not highly traded tend to be rather difficult to trade because there are usually very few sellers and buyers available. Also, stocks with low liquidity are usually poorly priced, sometimes at less than a penny for each share. This is risky as they can be manipulated by investors.

Examine the charts

Experts advise that traders closely examine the chart of the stock they intend to buy as part of the technical analysis. When you examine the charts, you need to spot the bottom and identify the best entry points. You must also examine the ceiling in order to identify the ideal exit points. All investors purchase stocks hoping the price will almost immediately go up. It is, therefore, crucial to look at and understand historical chart patterns of the particular stock.

The buy point can be perceived as the ground floor of a building where an elevator is about to rise to new heights. You must not only buy the right stock at the right price but also at the right time.

'Cup with handle' pattern

One of the most effective patterns that allow consistency with purchasing stocks is the 'cup with handle' pattern. This is the point where you buy a stock at its lowest price because it's likely to rise very fast. Human nature is still the same, even traders and other big players in the markets exhibit either greed or fear.

What is the 'buy point?'

This is defined as the price level where a stock is very likely to rise significantly. The 'buy point,' also known as an 'entry point,' is a point in the chart that offers the least resistance to a price increase.

Example

The 'cup without a handle' is an approach that worked for a long time. It is still believed to be among the most successful strategies for determining entry points. Let us take a stock that has seen its price decline by up to 33%. This is after a successful upward trend that showcased an all-time high.

However, for 6 weeks, the stock starts to decline. But, once the decline is over and the upward trend begins, there are no signs of a major pullback. At this level, the entry point is pretty simple to determine. It is identified to be 10 cents on top of the peak towards the left-hand side. As soon as the stock recovers and gains 10 cents on top of the previous highest level. It is at this point that you enter the trade.

Chapter 7: Read Charts, Use Indicators & Watch Markets

How to read charts

There are numerous types of stock charts. Examples of these charts include candlestick charts, line charts, point-and-figure, open-high-low-close charts, bar charts and many others. These charts are viewable in varying time frames. For instance, we have weekly, daily, intraday, and even monthly charts.

There are advantages and downsides of each chart type and time frame. They can be applied in different situations. What they reveal include price and volume action which are extremely important to traders and investors.

Why are stock charts valuable?

When you find a share that you think has strong fundamentals, the next step is to look at its charts. The stock chart will provide you with useful insights that will guide you on the best time to enter a trade, how long you should stay in the trade, and when to exit.

Charts often plot both volume and price data in a format that is easy to read. This way, you can easily spot entry and exit points. The key metrics to look out for are volume and price.

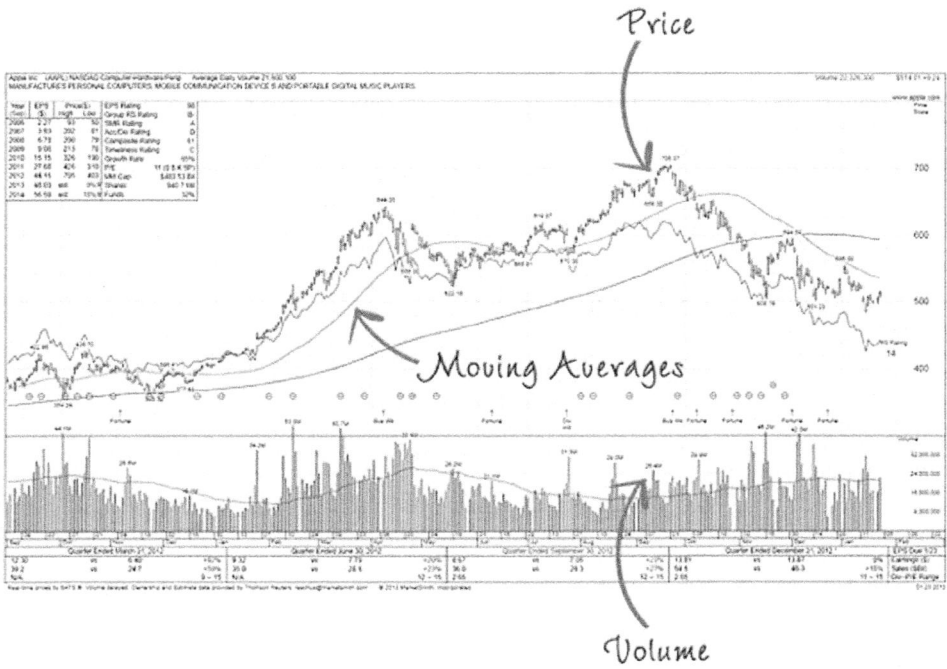

Price

Moving Averages

Volume

Stock chart interpretation

Price

On the stock chart above, there are marks colored magenta and blue. These marks represent the stock's price history. The volumes are also represented on the chart. The bars represent the price. The length of the vertical bars on the charts indicates a stock's price range. Therefore, the top of the bar indicates the highest price paid in that specific time period while the bottom of the bar indicates the lowest stock price paid.

The tiny intersecting lines that run horizontally, point to the closing price at the end of the particular trading period. When the bar is in blue, this implies that stock price is equal to or greater than the previous price. However, it will be represented by magenta if it is less than the previous price.

Volumes

At the bottom of the chart are vertical lines. These vertical lines represent the volume of shares traded within the indicated period of time. The height of the volume bars represents a value that is similar to that indicated on the right-hand side scale.

The color of the bars is determined by the preceding price bar. The bar color is blue if the price is greater than or equal to the previous period's last price. The color is magenta if the price is lower than the previous period's final price.

Moving averages

Moving averages are indicated on stock charts in order to smooth out price data through the creation of one flowing line. This line basically represents the average price within a given time frame. Volatility is smoothed out by the moving average line. This makes it easier to spot points of convergence and divergence on a well-established price trend.

Traders and investors prefer to see moving averages that trend upwards. They also prefer to have a stock's current price, closing higher than the trading average. This way, a trader or investor will be confident that the stock is headed in the right direction.

There is a clear red line that cut across the volume bars. This is another moving average line, specifically the 50-day moving average. The line is derived by adding together the total of volumes traded in the past 50 days and then dividing it by 50.

Comparing stocks market indices

Investors use stock market indices as a general measure of how the stocks or securities markets are faring on any given day. Let us assume that you are a trader and your portfolio of securities is headed south. If the indices are also on a downward trend, then you can assume that lethargy and pessimism are present in the general economy.

However, if your portfolio is underperforming while the indices are on an upward trend, then you may wish to reconsider some of your investments. The health of the stock market is often measured using different market indices. If the economy is faring well, then the indices will rise. However, if the economy is depressed, then the markets will follow suit and the indices will be on a downward trend.

Two popular stock market indices

The two best known and most popular stock market indices are the Standard and Poor's 500 Index and the Dow Jones Industrial Average (DJIA). These two indices are popularly known as the benchmark of the securities market. They are both important because they provide an indication of the wellbeing of the securities market. They also give traders and investors a historic basis that they can rely on to gain invaluable insights into the goings-on in the markets and also derive useful data.

The DJIA is made up of 30 US companies with large market capitalization. The S&P 500 represents 500 major firms that have huge market capitalization and are usually selected by a committee. We also have the NASDAQ 100. This index consists of both US and international large-cap firms, but not any from the financial services sector.

How to conduct the comparison

1. Determine the indices you wish to compare

   We have observed that there are 2 major indices as well as NASDAQ. Each of the indices fares differently so one may be down while the others are up and so on.

2. **Note that there are other smaller indices**

   There are numerous types of stock indices across the different markets. Some of the smaller ones include the Dow Jones Transport Average. Some are industry-specific so choose the indices you wish to compare carefully.

3. Choose your preferred time frame

    Basically, the components of a particular index are likely to change based on a number of factors. The price is also likely to change so consider the time frame that you are interested in.

4. **Check out charting sites and compare prices**

    There are websites that contain the prices of different stocks and shares, like Yahoo Finance. You will get the information that you need regarding specific stock market indices. Other websites where you can find charts with indices include:

    - www.smartmoney.com
    - www.fool.com
    - www.bigchart.com

    Once you get to the charts, find the advanced chart feature for one index then enter the symbol of the index you wish to compare.

Conclusion

Thank you for making it through to the end of this book, let's hope it was informative and that it provided you with all of the tools you need to achieve your goals whatever they may be.

The next step is to start trading on a simulated trader and apply the strategies you've learned in this book. Make sure that you practice all the useful lessons that are found here. This is a proven approach that will turn you into a pro in just a short period of time.

We are sure that this book has opened your eyes to the rigors of swing trading and how you can become a successful swing trader yourself. If you follow these strategies carefully and apply them diligently, then there is no doubt that you will improve your skills and thrive in your swing trading career.

Finally, if you found this book useful in any way, a review on Amazon is always appreciated!

Stock Market Investing for Beginners:

The Best Book on Stock Investments

To Help You Make Money

In Less Than 1 Hour a Day

Table of contents

Description

befitting its nature, it is presented without assurance regarding its prolonged validity or interim quality. Trademarks that are mentioned are done without written consent and can in no way be considered an endorsement from the trademark holder.

Introduction

The stock market refers to all the parties involved in the buying and selling of shares of publicly listed companies, bonds, and other securities. It is a vital component of the free economy. It consists of two main segments: the primary market and the secondary market.

The primary market is made up of mainly early-stage companies seeking resources through the sale of shares in what is known as IPOs. Thanks to the stock market, companies may acquire funds by selling stock to public investors in exchange for part ownership.

The market is on an upward trajectory and more investors are turning to stocks. This implies that the stock market is an incredibly profitable niche. Actually, the third richest man in the world, Warren Buffett, made his fortune through investing in the stock market. But the main difference between Warren Buffett and other investors is down to discipline and rationality.

Making money from the stock market is not as hard as people make it out to be. Like any other field, it can be mastered, and the only real way of mastering stock markets is through study and practice. Many investors make a killing out of stock markets. In the same vein, many investors commit their resources to bad investments and lose it all.

The stock market can be a very unforgiving pursuit, and in order to realize a profit, you must be armed with not just pedestrian investment tips, but solid information.

This book details all the basics of stock market investing and shows you how to get started.

Part 1: The Essentials of Stock Market Investment

Chapter 1:

Investment vs. Speculation

In the 1934 classic book, *Security Analysis*, Ben Graham says, *"An investment operation is one which, upon thorough analysis, promises safety of principal and a satisfactory return. Operations not meeting these requirements are speculative."*

In simple terms, an investor is a person who determines to make their money work for them. For instance, they may use their savings to purchase, a percentage of a company, and thus be entitled to a share of the company's profits for as long as they retain ownership.

The average employee must work for their money. They exchange their time and skills for money. Unlike employees, money doesn't tire, doesn't catch an illness, doesn't develop moods, or doesn't get bored, and so it has the distinction of having a 24-hour utility. An investor should know how to put money into use in such a manner that it will earn him great returns.

An often-prevalent misconception is that investing is a preserve of the high and mighty. It's true that millionaires and billionaires are into it, but it doesn't mean that it is *their* preserve. Any person who has a reasonable amount of cash is a very good candidate for being an investor. But like anywhere else, investing has its rules, and it's only the people who stick to the rules who end up beating the system.

When you fail to act within the rules of investing, you might unbeknownst to you become a mere speculator. A speculator is interested in only short gains. Speculators are proverbially carried by the wind and they tend to rush in markets where they can make a killing in as short amount of time as possible. For this reason, speculators are vulnerable, and they constantly fall prey to market frauds. For instance, in mid-2017, the price of a cryptocurrency known as Bitcoin had experienced an artificially engineered surge, and some speculators went so far as to even sell their property and buy bitcoin in hopes of making a massive overnight return. They hadn't known that they were getting sucked into a bubble, but soon enough, the bubble blew up, and the lofty dreams of all of those speculators came crashing down. An ocean of tears was shed and lives were ruined.

The father of value investing, Ben Graham, said, "There are many ways in which speculation may be unintelligent. Of these, the foremost are: (1) speculating when you think you're investing; (2) speculating seriously instead of as a pastime when you lack proper knowledge and skill for it; and (3) risking more money in speculation than you can afford to lose."

The main obligation of an investor is to analyze in detail the long-term potential of a particular business endeavor and then decide whether to commit their resources into that endeavor. The goal of every investor is to earn a good return on their investment.

Some of the popular long-term investments include:

- **Stocks**

- **Bonds**

- **Mutual funds**

- **ETFs**

- **Alternative investments**

Chapter 2:
Understanding the Stock Market

The stock market plays a critical role in driving the economy. It is characterized by the trading of equities of publicly listed companies and other securities. A popular investment style sees investors pumping their funds into a public company in exchange for part or full ownership of the company. Thus, the investors are entitled to a share of the company profits. In this vein, a successful investor is one that receives more in the way of dividends than the capital they initially gave out. The stock market is divided into two categories, namely, primary and secondary capital markets.

Primary market: this is where shares or equities are traded via an initial public offering (IPO) i.e. investors trade directly with the company.

Secondary market: investors trade among themselves while the company associated with the traded security is excluded from the trading.

The two factors that determine the price of a public company's IPO stock are the value of the company and the volume of shares.

The company may stash away its IPO windfall, but once its stock trading grows enough to generate revenue, the company doesn't profit. The stock trading of most companies is normally carried out on exchanges. Exchanges play the role of facilitating trade between buyers and sellers. Thanks to new technology, exchanges now list stocks in electronic format.

Stock market exchanges are found in almost any capital city in the world. In the U.S., there are two major stock exchanges: the **New York Stock Exchange** and the **Nasdaq.**

The Securities and Exchange Commission, an independent federal agency, oversees the exchanges in the U.S. to enforce fair play and protect the rights of the investors.

Investors who are constrained by cash, usually thrive in exchanges as opposed to IPOs. IPOs prefer working with large investment vehicles (for instance Berkshire Hathaway) as opposed to small two-thousand-in-the-bank investors. But the exchanges welcome anyone to purchase securities. Investors may get in on the action themselves or they might hire brokers.

The stock price is driven by supply and demand forces. For instance, if there's a lot of buzz around a company, and there are lots people wanting to buy shares of that company, the share price will go up, and the same is true for profitable companies too.

Types of shares:

- **Ordinary shares**

- **B-Ordinary shares**

- **N-Ordinary shares**

- **Preference shares**

- **Exchange traded funds**

The two primary types of securities traded on the stock market are **listed securities** and **over-the-counter** (OTC). Listed securities must meet the requirements of the exchange and must also receive approval from the Securities and Exchange Commission.

On the other hand, over-the-counter securities are traded between peers, where the trades are usually facilitated by dealers. Over-the-counter securities don't appear on exchanges and they don't have to fulfill SEC requirements.

There's always an underlying element of risk in investments. You risk losing it all or not making as much profit as you had anticipated. Warren Buffett, the legendary investor, warned that risk came from not knowing enough.

Reading financial journals, attending investor workshops, and hiring professionals are some of the techniques you can use to minimize or eliminate risk from your decision.

Some products and securities are riskier than others. For instance, cash in the bank, government bonds, and ETFs are considered to have low risk, whereas corporate bonds, shares, and derivatives are considered high-risk. On the brighter side, a high-risk investment has the potential of being exceedingly profitable. The best protective measure against failure is to diversify. A diverse investment portfolio helps you absorb the loss and also speeds up wealth creation.

The main players in the stock market include:

- **Stockbrokers**

- **Stock analysts**

- **Investment bankers**

- **Portfolio managers**

Chapter 3:

Make More Money and Take Fewer Risks with Mutual Funds

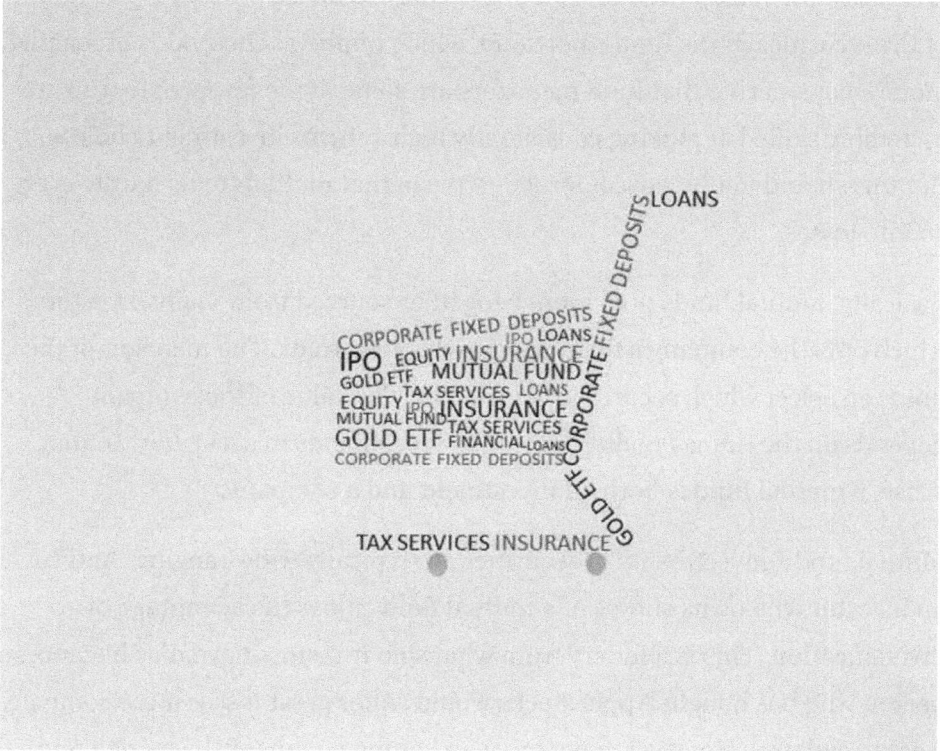

Mutual funds appeal to investors who have the mind of unity as opposed to striking it alone. Mutual funds are high-flying projects in which resources are pooled together for the purpose of a scaled securities investment. The funds are contributed by investors in exchange for a slice of ownership of the fund. The fund is directed by qualified personnel known as a fund manager. The investment decisions are made by the manager, with the board acting as the authorizing body. Generally, a mutual fund must have goals, and it is upon the fund manager to ensure that they realize these goals.

The shares of mutual funds are bought at the fund's present Net Asset Value (NAV). This value is arrived at by dividing the securities value of the total shares. Having a stake in a mutual fund is a much more secure and rewarding investment than purchasing shares of random companies. Mutual funds give the "small investor" an opportunity to own a portion of the value of the securities in the fund's portfolio, which improves their odds of making money, considering that fund managers are some of the few people who are incredibly skilled at making consistently high-returns investment choices. But this should not be misconstrued to mean that mutual funds hardly ever go into losses.

Basically, mutual funds pool money together sourced from many investors, which puts the company's financial muscle on steroids. The manager of the fund can select which securities to invest in. The value of the company depends on the tidings realized from the investments in securities. In that sense, a mutual fund is both an investment and a company.

Mutual funds' investments in securities are typically wide-ranging. And so, an investor who owns shares of a mutual fund enjoys the advantage of diversification. This is a far cry from what solo investors have. For instance, a person who has bought Apple stocks would suffer great losses if the company were to collapse. However, a person who has ownership of shares of a mutual fund is likely to emerge unscathed when their company makes a loss from a specific investment because their company holds a wide range of investments.

Types of mutual funds:

- Fixed income

- Index funds

- Balanced funds

- Money market funds

- Sector funds

- Equity funds

- Alternative funds

- Smart-beta funds

- Target-date funds

- Funds-of-funds

A fund normally distributes its income to shareholders over the year. The shareholders have the option of receiving cold cash or reinvesting. Here are the three ways in which a mutual fund investor earns:

- They may receive shareholder dividends and the interest on bonds.

- If the fund sells its securities at a higher price, part of the income generated is distributed amongst shareholders.

- If the value of the fund goes up as a result of investment in securities, the fund's share prices go up too, in that way an investor would sell their shares at a higher price.

Reasons why investing in mutual funds are far better than purchasing stock:

Professional management. The average investor probably has no time, skills, and information to make an educated investment decision. But a mutual fund is controlled by an able manager who should make the best decisions on your behalf.

Diversification. Mutual funds invest in a wide range of securities, thus spreading the risk.

Economies of scale. A mutual fund buys and sells in large volumes and so they are entitled to reduced fees. Also, a mutual fund has the capacity to invest in big proportions as opposed to what a single person could have managed.

Simple. In this age of technology, buying a mutual fund is a few clicks away.

Transparency. They are regulated.

Ease of access. Mutual funds can be purchased and sold with ease on exchanges.

Custom. An investor has the liberty to scout for a mutual fund that aligns with him even philosophically.

Chapter 4:
What are Index Funds and ETFs?

An *index* refers to the collective securities that represent the value of an economic sector. Investors track indices in order to determine how well or badly a market sector is doing.

An *index fund* is a collection of securities investments that involves tracking of market performance. Investors gain when the market goes up. Index funds are a viable investment path because they offer wide exposure in the market and considerably lower expenses, as opposed to, for instance, hedge funds.

As a form of passive fund management, index funds sometimes bring more gains than the highly bureaucratic mutual funds. The majority of index funds track the S&P 500.

Before purchasing an index fund, an investor should first understand the index, and also check the rate in which an index fund replicates the gains of its index. Although an index fund is considered a passive form of investing, it is upon the portfolio manager to say how the fund will track the index.

Some funds may seek gains from an index by investing in the constituent securities of that index, while other funds may seek gains by purchasing securities that appear similar to the securities within its index, and moreover, some funds may replicate an index by use of other financial instruments.

An *exchange-traded-fund* (ETF) is a collection of securities investments whose shares may be purchased or sold on an exchange at the set market price. An ETF is similar to a mutual fund in the sense that it collects resources from many investors and then invests in the best-performing markets. An ETF must have an investment goal and a sense of direction.

Most ETFs only ever invest in securities and must operate within the guidelines set by the Securities and Exchange Commission (SEC).

Types of ETFs:

- Broad market

- Sector and industry

- International

- Commodities

- Currency

- Dividend and income

- Fixed income/bonds

- Passive or active management

- Leveraged or hedged strategies

- Factor-based strategies

- Capitalization-weighted

ETFs are listed on exchanges and you may purchase or sell shares during trading hours. The price of ETF is determined by market forces, unlike mutual funds whose share prices are determined by the Net Asset Value (NAV) which is calculated at the close of the trading day.

Benefits of ETFs:

- You may buy ETFs through your broker at any time during trading hours.

- ETFs promotes portfolio diversification. ETFs confers securities to investors in various sectors, markets, and asset classes.

- The operating fees are significantly lower than mutual fund and hedge fund fees.

- ETFs are highly liquid partly due to their quick tradability on exchanges.

- ETFs has accurate price tracking.

Important things to evaluate before investing in an ETF:

- Objectives

- Risks

- Costs

An ETF generally has an objective that it proudly states. It is upon you to judge whether the strategies that the sponsor employs are worthy or not.

As a securities investment pool, ETFs carry an element of risk. The main risks are associated with uncontrollable factors, for instance, market failure, currency fluctuations or inflation. But also watch out that you don't fall prey to scams!

Some of the fees associated with ETFs include:

- Administrative

- Advisory

- Fund operating expenses

- Brokerage commissions

- Bids

- Premium/discount volatility

Chapter 5:

Secrets of Investing in IPOs

An *initial public offering* (IPO) is a popular method of raising investment capital and it involves a company selling its stock to the public for the first time. IPOs are commonly sought by early-stage companies in order to gain capital for expanding their operations. IPOs may also be sought by private companies that want to become publicly traded, thus the common phrase, "Going public."

IPOs offer the common public a chance to own the company. Prior to the issuance of an IPO, a company is considered private, since the people holding a stake in the company are likely a compact group consisting of founders and angel investors.

Some of the reasons a company goes public include:

- Access to greater funds.

- It promotes a more liquid and diverse share capital base.

- It strengthens brand image and credibility.

- Puts the company in a position to acquire other companies in the future.

- There's a higher valuation due to the release of documents and elimination of uncertainty.

- Provides liquidity for investors.

- Rewards its performing management through share options.

- Fosters the company's competitive edge.

- Debt reduction opportunity.

For an average investor, buying stock from a company may be a rarity, but still, some investors luck out. To understand why it is a rarity, you have to remember that a company's interest is raising about as much money as it possibly can. And so, a company would rather get the big-buck institutions to buy stock rather than thousands of investors. Selling a million shares to an institution is way more efficient than finding thousands of investors to buy shares. Also, many investors lose out on a chance to invest in IPOs because the brokers that the company works with are more likely to "take the deal" to the investors in their circles.

In this way, your chances of getting in on the IPO action result in a big part on having a well-connected broker with whom you're in good standing. Brokers tend to have many clients and they may be biased against some of their clients. Beyond this, you could also try to approach the founders of a company and request for a consideration in IPO offers.

But simply because you have a chance to invest in IPOs doesn't automatically mean that you will earn a profit. Take some of these measures to get out of harm's way.

Be cautious. If your broker asks you to invest in a certain IPO, don't just run for it like a madman, but take your time to see that it is the right decision.

Vet the top management. If the executives are newsmakers in a negative light, time to boot. You can't commit your monies to someone who, for instance, rapes interns.

Go for the big fish. Big firms have an image to protect but the small fish couldn't care less.

Do your research. It can be hard finding information about a company that is going public. But that doesn't excuse the fact that you must dig hard enough and uncover relevant information touching upon the company's inner workings, financial health, and business practices. Research brings up stuff that either solidifies your interest or puts you off.

Read the prospectus. It is not the most interesting stuff to read, but you should go through it if only to understand the company's direction, risks, and opportunities.

Part 2: Maximize Returns from your Stock Selection

Chapter 6:
How to Make Money from Fundamental Analysis

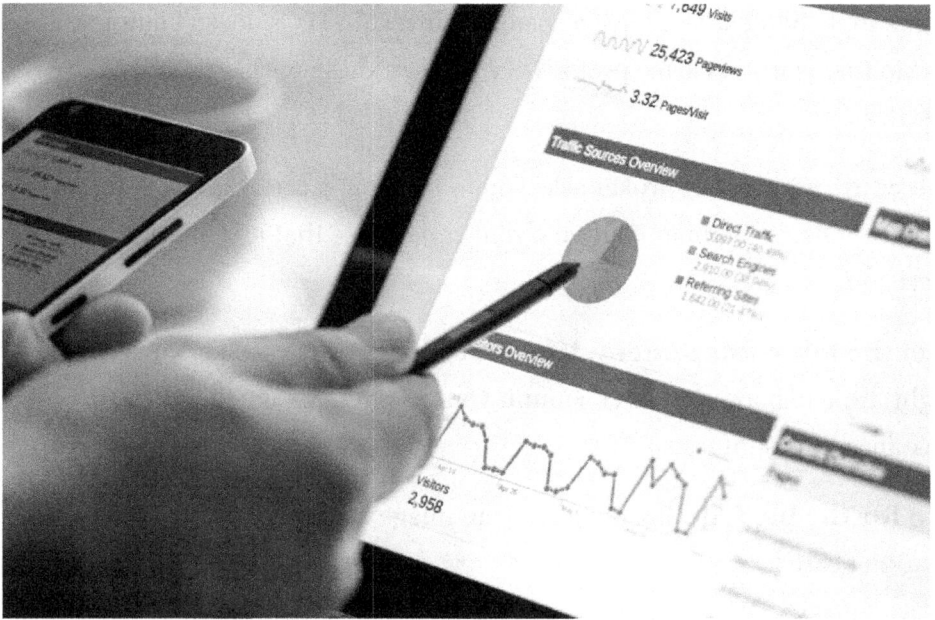

Fundamental analysis is the study of the fiscal data of a company. The aim is to determine the financial health and performance of a company, as well as project, whether a company will be strong or weak in the future. Fundamental analysis is a critical financial exercise because it empowers the investor and helps them decide whether or not to invest. It is **fundamental** to success in securities investing.

Fundamental analysis could be employed in any kind of securities valuation, although most investors tend to confine it in stock valuation. Some of the key metrics taken into account include income, profit margins, interest rates and projected future growth.

A thorough evaluation of the financial statements of a company helps to draw an accurate conclusion.

An investor who is proficient at making fundamental analysis has an unfair advantage over the rest. Warren Buffett, also known as the Oracle of Omaha, made his incalculable fortune through buying off companies that he estimated would be successful in the future. But what made his predictions so accurate? It is an open secret that fundamental analysis would help him arrive at these decisions.

Interestingly, some investors use shallow and unscientific techniques to evaluate companies' performance, overlooking a time-tested method like fundamental analysis. The reasons for this might be that they lack the skill or time or even the concern, which is a mistake. The initial effort required at the start of making an investment is usually larger, but thereafter one is rewarded with a passive income.

It is important to have the tools for fundamental analysis in order to look beyond the results at face-value. The tools extrapolate on market value, earnings, and growth. Some of the most important factors to consider include:

Earnings per share. What percentage of profit is assigned to the shares?

Price-to-earnings ratio. What is the current share price to its earnings per share?

Projected earnings growth. By what percentage will the stock grow within an annual time-frame?

Price-to-sales ratio. What is the share price compared to the revenue of the corporation?

Price-to-book ratio. What is the book value of the stock compared to its market value?

Dividend payout ratio. What is the number of dividends paid out to shareholders compared to the company's income?

Dividend yield. What are the yearly dividends compared to stock prices?

Return on equity. What is the company's return on equity? This figure is found by dividing a company's net income by stockholders' equity.

Always remember that these numbers play the role in shaping your judgment and must be used wholly, not disjointly, and are thus a yardstick for measuring the income-potential of a particular investment.

It is a better idea to wade through the waters of security's, investing guided by something more than just your gut feeling: fundamental analysis. Even if you perceive yourself as illiterate in matters of finance, you must not allow that attitude to hold you back from becoming your own stock market analyst.

While fundamental analysis focuses on securities valuation by studying financial statements of a company, technical analysis merely study market forces and their impact on securities value.

Chapter 7:

Quick Due Diligence, Medium Due Diligence, and Full Due Diligence

Due diligence is the process of vetting the authenticity of an investment. It is made in order to eliminate debt from the parties to a transaction. Due diligence is normally carried out when there's a deal on the table, but the parties to that deal have not sealed a contract yet.

In the world of securities investments, due diligence is carried out by fund managers, brokers, stock analysts, and investors. It is a highly recommended operation for investors. You get to assess the value of an investment and weigh the associated risks. Also, you get served with important company documents that may reveal insider information that would not have been otherwise available.

An investor should have a list of metrics to check against. Here's a sample checklist:

A) FINANCIAL INFORMATION

1. Annual and quarterly fiscal information

- Income statements, cash flows, and balance sheets

- Plans vs. results

- Financial reports of management

- Sales and profit breakdown by location, type of product, and channel

- Customer backlog

- Accounts receivable

2. Economic performance projections

- Quarterly economic performance projections: revenue and income statements.

- The major drivers of growth and prospects

- Business predictability

- Foreign operations risk e.g. national instability

- The pricing policies of industry and company

- The economic assumptions

- Capital expenditure projections and capital arrangements

- External finance

3. Capital structure

- Outstanding shares

- Shareholder list

- Debt instruments

- Liabilities off balance sheet

4. Other information

- Tax positions

- Operating loss

- Accounting policies

- Relevant financing history

B) PRODUCTS

1. Product description

- Major applications

- The growth rate projected

- Market share

- Nature and speed of technological change

- Product timing and enhancement

- Profitability and cost structure

C) INFORMATION ABOUT CUSTOMERS & SUPPLIERS

1. Top customers' name, location and address

2. Customers' relationship quality

3. Customers' individual revenue

4. Meaningful relationships that broke apart

5. Suppliers' list

6. Suppliers' relationship quality

D) COMPETITION

1. Landscape of competition in each segment

- Competition basis

- Market position

E) SALES, MARKETING AND DISTRIBUTION

1. Strategy

- Local and international distribution channels

- Company products and positioning

- Market opportunities

- Associated risks

- Marketing programs

2. Customers

- Relationship statuses and trends

- Future growth prospects and development

- Analysis

3. Main ways of generating new business

4. Model of productivity

- New workers

- Cycle of sales

- Compensation

5. Market plan implementation within given budget

F) RESEARCH AND DEVELOPMENT

1. Organization description

- Main activities

- Principals

- strategies

2. New products

- Timing and status

- Development costs

- Important technologies

- Associated risks

G) PERSONNEL AND MANAGEMENT

1. Management chart

2. Personnel numbers by location and role

3. Detailed profiles of senior management

4. Compensation plans

5. Management's incentive options

6. Important employee relations

7. Turnover of personnel

H) LEGAL MATTERS

1. Company lawsuits by aggrieved

2. Lawsuits filed by company

3. Environmental issues

4. Employee issues

5. Company liabilities

6. Intellectual property

- Copyrights

- Licenses

- Trademarks

7. Insurance cover

8. History of trouble with governing bodies e.g. Securities and Exchange Commission

Chapter 8:

Computation of Investment and Profitability Ratios

Whenever an investor commits their resources to an investment project, their intention is to generate a profit. The gains that an investor earns from an investment are known as return on investment (ROI).

Return on investment can be projected, too. A computation model is used to work out the projected gains and divides the gains by the original investment sum, thus finding the ratio.

ROI or return ratio is critical in helping an investor realize how their securities investments are stacked against the stock market. Investors like a simple metric for evaluating stock performance and profitability.

Profit is the income earned less the expenses, and it can be worked out in many different ways. A profit is the principal reason companies exist. A company that is profitable is assured of sticking around while a company that sustains a loss for a long time is likely to go out of business. ROI is what investors use to gauge their performance, and as an investor, it is always prudent to take action from reports where your investments are concerned, otherwise your investment career is at risk of going up in flames.

For instance, if Tim put $1500 of his savings into Milly's Computers, Inc. in 2017 and then sold his stock in 2018 for $2000 to get his return on investment, he would divide his profit ($500) by the initial investment sum ($1500) to get 33%.

Supposing that Tim had invested in other business projects, he might use the ROI from his investment in Milly's Computers, Inc. as a benchmark of the performance of his other investments.

Due to some limitations of the ROI method, some experts have proposed taking into account the social returns that an investment confers on an investor. This theory was developed in the early 2000s and it connects investments to social and environmental factors.

Margin ratios

- **Gross profit margin.** This metric allows investors to gauge a company's health by working out the money left over from income less cost of goods sold.

- **Operating margin.** This shows how much money is left over after deducting both cost of goods and operating expenses.

- **Net profit margin.** This is arrived at after deducting operating expenses, preferred stock dividends, interest, and taxes, from a company's revenue.

- **Operating cash flow margin.** A common method of working out profitability ratios, this margin indicates the money gained out of an investment activity per every dollar in sales.

Returns ratios

- **Return on assets.** This shows the company profits compared to company assets.

- **Return on equity.** This method works out how many dollars in profit a company makes with each dollar of stockholders' equity.

- **Cash return on assets.** A ratio that is used in comparing the performance of a business against other businesses in the industry. It is worked out by dividing the cash from investment operations of the company's total average assets.

The failure rate in companies is excessively high. And so, an investor ought to be very adept at researching companies and coming up with an accurate future valuation. An investor who's convinced that an investment has no capacity for profit is better off staying away from that investment.

Part 3: Strategies for Stock Market Investment

Chapter 9:

Winning Strategies of Investing in Stocks, Forex, Commodities, and Indices

Every successful investment management company has a hallowed business philosophy, but no matter how great their strategies are, there can never be a win-win situation unless you play your part well. There are many investment dynamics that are well within the control of an investor.

The average investor never appears concerned about playing his part well, especially if he has a broker or if he invests primarily in funds. He might express worry about the markets, the economy, manager popularity, or securities performances—which are greater things to worry about, actually—

but when he fails to play his role, he lessens the momentum of everyone involved.

Folks, you have got to realize that there's no magic bullet, no one special trick that is going to eliminate all risk and guarantee you sky-high profits. The only way of reducing risk is by being competent. And you become competent through consuming relevant information and practicing.

The winning strategies are actually the default roles of an investor.

Goal. An investor should have a goal in mind. A great goal is both measurable and within reach. A goal should be well-defined and realistic, and a path should be outlined for it. If an investor has no plan they will approach an investment piecemeal rather than push the entire portfolio for a common objective.

Balance. An investor should allocate assets using widely diversified funds. The asset allocation should fit into the portfolio's objective. The intelligent investor commits their resources on a number of business projects, thus spreading the risk. With a wide portfolio, the process of wealth creation becomes easier.

Minimize costs. The lower your costs, the bigger your share of returns. And research has shown that many low-cost investments have done better than higher-cost investments. An example of a lower-cost investment is purchasing index funds, which have a lower operating cost as compared to hedge funds and mutual funds.

Have discipline. This one cannot be overstated. When you invest, you might become vulnerable, especially when there is market turmoil. Investors react to shock-news by making impulsive investment decisions. You want to guard against that impulsivity. It'd be difficult to watch yourself without discipline. In as much as many people are killing it in the stock market, there are also others who are getting thrown down and stomped on, never rising again, and one would argue they lack discipline.

Evaluate your tax options. When you invest in funds, it is critical to assess your tax options. Always calculate the impact of taxes on your returns. The amount of tax levied will be affected by the type of your investment. Investing in funds attracts much more tax than purchasing shares.

Avoid mainstream media. Warren Buffett, the richest investor, spends his day reading books. He doesn't spend his day flipping from one channel to another, exposing his mind to the toxic world news. You might want to borrow a leaf from him. The mainstream media are negative on purpose. They aim to evoke people's emotions. You might consume too much negative media about the stock market and end up misleading yourself or even worse developing a negative outlook.

Fundamental analysis. Warren Buffett, again, the world's most successful investor is big on fundamental analysis, so why not you? Some people opt out of fundamental analysis on the complaint of not having a background in finance, failing to recognize that they could learn the concept or hire an expert. It has been said that fundamental analysis is fundamental to being able to make money in the stock market.

Chapter 10:
Principles of Value Investing

Ben Graham, the father of value investing once said, *"The intelligent investor is a realist who sells to optimists and buys from pessimists."*

Value investing is an investment strategy where an investor finds stocks that trade for less than their intrinsic value. Value investors vigorously look for stocks that they consider undervalued by the market. The idea is to swoop in early enough so that by the time a market segment awakens to the intrinsic value of the stock, the value investor will stand to make a large return on investment. Warren Buffett has made an incredibly large fortune out of being an excellent value investor.

Value investing varies from one person to another. Two investors can have wildly differing opinions on a similar investment. Some value investors tend to look at earnings and assets and place no value on projected future growth. Other value investors (Warren Buffett types) base their plans on future development of the company.

An illustration of the subjectivity of value investment:

On January 5, 2017, Glenn & Waters, Inc. released its Q1 2017 earnings report. Later, there was a steep decline in trading, which cost the company 19% of its value.

The company earned $500 million in the first quarter of 2017, which was a 50% rise from a year ago. The projected earnings of the company in the 2nd quarter of the year are $540 million.

The company is obviously healthy economic-wise and has great room for growth. However, since the company had a lot of development and research costs paid out in the 1st quarter of the year, earnings per share went down in comparison to the previous year.

Noticing this, some investors jump at the opportunity, selling off enough stock to cause a dip in share prices. All the while, a value investor understands that Glenn & Waters, Inc. is an undervalued company, with the potential of flourishing in the future.

Companies carry an intrinsic value. A value investor's main duty is to scout for companies that may be considered "weak" at present but in their assessment, these companies have a bright future. So, a value investor determines to work out the intrinsic value of the company.

Margin of safety. This is the difference between a stock's intrinsic value and its current market value. A value investor who purchases undervalued stock obviously gets entitled to a wide margin of safety in the event that stock prices go up, and yet they are unlikely to suffer a loss when the market doesn't perform as they'd hoped.

The efficient-market hypothesis is inaccurate. The efficient-market hypothesis states that all the relevant information about a company is reflected in its stock performance, and for that reason, there are no loopholes to beat the market. A value investor understands that a company's stock may sometimes be overvalued or undervalued. It is upon him to seek out the undervalued companies.

Never follow the herd. As Warren Buffett aptly said, "We simply attempt to be fearful when others are greedy and to be greedy only when others are fearful." The value investor bucks the trend.

Patience is important. A value investor never goes around devouring anything in his path. He understands that undervalued companies with a high intrinsic value don't come by easily. And so he waits until the appropriate company shows up in his radar.

Volatility is not necessarily risky. It may very well complement the value investment approach.

Chapter 11:

Margin of Safety and Competitive Edge in Growth Investment

Warren Buffett once said, "The three most important words in investing are 'margin of safety.'"

The margin of safety is the one thing that value investors are after, but what is it? The margin of safety is the difference between the market value of a stock and its intrinsic value. The margin of safety is found in undervalued investments that flourish at a later time.

Intrinsic value is the projected worth of an investment. It comprises an investment's estimated growth rate, future cash flow, and risk.

Working out the intrinsic value of an investment is not as easy as it may first seem. There are many variables that come into play. But the difficulty varies from one security to another. For instance, it is easier to calculate the intrinsic value of a bond than that of equity stock. The cash flow and duration of a bond is fixed. A stock has many variables that play a key role in its future performance. Generally, stocks call for a bigger margin of safety than bonds.

The main purpose of working out the intrinsic value is so as to profit from the undervalued assets. As it happens in these cases, the market value of an asset is down, and it encourages an investor to commit his resources to the investment. However, if the market value of an asset is beyond its intrinsic value, an investor would pass on that, as it is obviously overvalued.

The required margin of safety is the price beneath the intrinsic value that an investor is willing to purchase the asset at. The farther away the market price is from the intrinsic value, the bigger the margin of safety.

The key to a good investment is not to judge how much the asset is going to affect people but rather how much it will grow. An investor must identify the competitive edge of a company and then figure out how long the edge is going to last.

Payback time is the amount of time that you get to wait to realize profits from your investment. The payback time may vary from a few months to years. Seasoned investors are in it for the long haul, and they mostly invest their money so as to see gains for years as opposed to chasing a quick buck.

A value investor minimizes risk by requiring a discount on the purchase of stock. This is because an inaccurate intrinsic value and a small margin of safety together make a highly risky investment. Ultimately, the combination of low risk and big safety margin make an investment very worthwhile.

Two versions of the safety margin:

- Budget-based

- Unit-based

A margin of safety may offer a cushion against inaccuracies, but it certainly does not guarantee that an investment will be successful. The methods of arriving at this seemingly mythical "intrinsic value" vary among different investment personnel.

Chapter 12:
Basics of Income Investing

Income investing means committing your resources on investments with the aim of drawing a steady income over a certain length of time. Bonds and CDs are historically popular income investment choices, but in recent years the returns have been dwindling, sending investors to other investment avenues like purchasing equity.

The rise of income investing can be attributed in part to the social unrest of the 20th century. In the 20th century, there was so much racism, hostility, cruelty, oppression of women and so on. These hostility tendencies necessitated creating a way in which someone would be in control of their own finances, and thus income investing came about.

And since the labor markets tended to favor white men only, people would survive by owning stocks of various products. These companies would send dividends to stockholders throughout the year based on their equity stake and how well the company had performed.

Types of income investments:

Equity income funds

Equity income funds score, particularly high amongst cash-strapped investors. They are a great way to diversify your portfolio away from cash and bonds.

Global equity income funds

A global equity income fund offers diversified access to many companies and capital markets for income and growth of capital.

Multi-asset income funds

They can generate income from various sources, which can be held directly or in funds, investing across bonds, cash, and rental property.

Investment trusts

These are structured companies run by a manager and hold various assets such as shares and bonds across the securities markets.

Fixed income

Fixed income investments such as bonds are hugely favored especially by investors who like regular payments over a fixed period of time.

Property

This asset class achieves real income growth over the course of time. For instance, a landlord increases rents and the price of a property goes up.

Stock

Both common stocks and preferred stocks are great investment choices. When you purchase stock in a company, you take a slice of ownership of the company. This entitles you to a share of the company profits known as dividends. Before you buy stock, you may want to check the dividend payout ratios as well as the frequency of payment.

Bonds

You have a vast pool to select from—agency bonds, government bonds, municipal bonds, and savings bonds. Your personal taxable equivalent yield gets to establish whether you buy corporate or municipal bonds. Buying bonds with maturation dates of 5 to 8 years puts you at duration risk.

Real estate

You can be an owner of rental property or you can invest in property through real estate investment trusts.

What should investors look for in dividend stocks for an income investment?

- A reasonable dividend ratio. Generally, an investor who invests $30 to the company should have generated positive income.

- The track-record should be on an upward trajectory.

- A high return on equity with zero company debt. These can help you understand how the people take to businesses.

Why avoid the real estate investment?

- If the market falls, the loss is increased by leverage.

- There's potential for a lot of obstruction like lawsuits, maintenance, and insurance.

- Stocks have always performed better long-term than real estate.

Chapter 13:

Stock Market Tips and Tricks

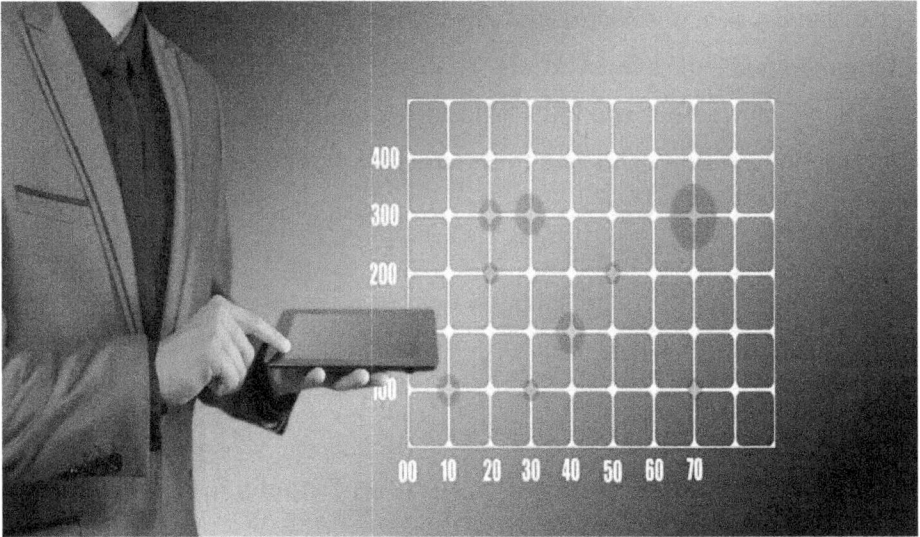

Right now, there are billions of dollars being generated throughout global stock markets. The stock markets are a very lucrative industry and at the same time very ruthless. It is a place where some men have made untold amounts of money while others have met their ruin.

Being successful in the stock market is not chalked to a fancy degree or the advice of your wealthy uncle. Stock markets reward knowledge and strategy.

Some people think that there's a quick buck to be made in trading stocks, and there's a name for them: speculators. Speculators often get burned when they try to play the system.

A great investor is not out to make a quick kill, but rather, he's there for the long haul. A great investor doesn't rush to eat anything that appears on his way. He's patient enough to wait for the fat calf which he will slaughter and eat to his fill.

No matter how skilled an investor might be, he too has a common enemy: risk. And one of the greatest favors he can do for himself is lowering the risk as much as possible.

Great investors know the value of discipline. Having discipline means not responding to news like a little puppy. It means not making impulsive decisions out of frustration. Having discipline amounts to operating within your guidelines and being true to yourself.

Stock market investment is not a reserve for the wealthy. Sure, there are many millionaires and billionaires throwing their monies into stock trading, but there's enough room for even "average investors."

Start early. Warren Buffett is the richest investor that ever lived. He made his first billion when he was well into his fifties. But the funny thing is that the Oracle of Omaha (Warren Buffett) had begun investing when he was a 10-year-old boy in Omaha. When you start early, you gain an unfair advantage over wide-eyed investors who come into stock trading a bit late.

Control the losses. Failing is a great part of moving forward. But don't fail so catastrophically that you cannot move any further ahead.

Check your emotions. Made a huge loss? Shut up. Made a fortune? Shut up. In truth, no one cares. Learn to not be overly emotional while reacting to market news.

Research is the secret. While most investors are happy taking wild rides and throwing their cash around and expect miracles, a great investor knows that investing is a hell of work, at least in the beginning, and heaviest part of it is doing research work. A great investor always researches on an investment first so that he may find as much information as need be before he finally reaches a decision. Knowing a hell lot about an investment certainly minimizes and even eliminates risk from the investment.

A great investor doesn't keep many balls in the air. They focus on a few high-value investments that are sure to give them enormous returns. When you juggle between a million investments, you end up losing your focus and becoming another victim of stock market ruthlessness.

Part 4: Stock Market Investment Approach

Chapter 14:

The Art of Short Selling

Short selling is the act of selling a security that one does not own. It is driven by the conviction that the security's value will go down over time and thus be able to be bought back to make a profit.

The equity-lending market plays the role of matching short sellers with stock owners willing to lend their shares at a cost. Apparently, there are many people who are interested in loaning out their shares and this industry is worth hundreds of billions!

Every investor wants to buy low and sell high. For instance, they may invest in stock, securities and wait for the price to go up. If they go up they may opt to sell their stock at a profit.

But there are times when markets experience strains that the stock price either dips or remains on a plateau. In these times, it is hard for an investor to make money taking advantage of the price difference.

And so, an investor may decide to borrow a security and sell it with the expectation of buying back shares later on at a reduced price to facilitate payment of the loan you'd taken.

Investors may short sell through brokerage firms. You place an order to sell the stock, and the broker inquires whether you are selling your own shares or short selling.

So, the brokerage allocates the investor's account shares borrowed from the market and then the sell order is executed. However, if the brokerage is unsuccessful in finding shares to loan your account, an investor will have to look in another market where loan-shares are available.

Once an investor sells the loaned shares, they wait for the security's price to lower, so they can buy the shares again at leverage. These newly bought shares are then returned to the original lender (through the broker) as loan payment, and you keep the difference as your earnings.

Stock exchanges have put in place regulations that discourage short selling shares that are moving down. And so, a short seller often finds himself swimming amongst the sharks.

Interestingly, the broker benefits of short selling when he charges transaction fees, but the actual owner of the shares might not even know that their shares had been loaned out.

Some of the risks associated with short selling include:

- **Short squeezes and "buy-ins."** A stock with high interest may experience price increment, which leads to unexpected losses on the part of the short seller.

- **Law.** Governing bodies might impose bans on short sellers in certain markets in order to prevent hysteria and protect the interests of traders. Such actions may cause a sudden rise in stock prices, thus the short seller sinks into losses.

- **Contrarian philosophy.** Short selling goes against the long-term market trend of prices moving up. Thus, a short seller is really gambling, and they have to execute the short selling at the most appropriate time.

In the long run, most stocks tend to drift up, not down, and with that in mind, short selling attempts to go against the general market direction, which can result in huge losses.

Chapter 15:

Buying on Margin

Buying on margin simply refers to the act of borrowing money to purchase securities. An investor typically pays the margin and then borrows the remaining amount from a financial institution.

Buying on margin is typically made a down payment to the broker, while the investor's securities act as collateral for the borrowed money. An investor must first open a margin account with a broker before buying on margin.

In the U.S., the governing bodies require that an investor purchase asset with at least 50% in cash and then they might seek borrowed funds for the other 50%.

Before an investor can buy on margin, the broker must, first of all, determine the minimum amount of equity that must be kept in their margin account, and also they must determine the percentage of the purchase price of securities that the investor must pay in cash.

If an investor puts down $20000, the maintenance margin is 50% or $10000. If the equity of the investor goes even a dollar below $10000, the broker should ask him to restore the equity to the agreed maintenance margin ($10000).

When an investor's account dips below the maintenance margin, the investor may restore their account to an acceptable maintenance margin by putting in more cash or selling securities bought with a loan.

Are there any benefits associated with buying on margin?

Buying on margin may have its benefits to investors, but the practice is also steeped in risk. Considering that an investor borrows money to finance the purchase of their securities, unless the value of these securities increases, an investor could suffer loss especially if the securities' value goes down. Knowing this, an investor should utilize their buy, on margin option with securities whose value they are sure will go up.

Another huge benefit of buying on margin is that an investor has more investing options. With a cash account, an investor can only buy stocks or have basic options strategies. But in an account with margin maintenance, an investor has the chance to even exploit bear markets, through engaging in short selling. Also, an investor may dabble in all types of stock option strategies, which give you the right to purchase or trade a hundred shares of an underlying stock at a set price.

Of course, short selling and options trading are steeped in a lot of risks, but on the flip side, they carry a lot of potential for making a profit. An inexperienced investor should probably stick to buying stock and waiting for the price to shoot up. However, it is totally okay when an experienced investor explores the options strategy and short selling strategy with the intention of making a big profit.

There's no single investment strategy that can be termed as the best. Ultimately, it comes down to your level of tolerance for risk and your investment knowledge. If you're a newbie, then investing with margin would be akin to committing financial suicide.

Also, it'd be helpful to call on a broker, because a broker is incredibly knowledgeable.

Chapter 16:

Strategies for Making High Profits and Reducing Risk in Day Trading

Day trading is the act of buying and selling financial instruments—whether once or many times over—in the same day and seeking to make a profit from the fluctuating price. Day trading has the potential of making a lot of money and in the same breath has a high risk of losing money.

The first step is to of course familiarize yourself with the basic trading procedures. Traders should be in-the-known about the latest market news and other events affecting the stock market. You should always read up on matters touching upon your stocks of interest.

As a day trader, you cannot eliminate the element of risk. And so, you have got to set aside a portion of your money that you can afford to lose. Most successful traders are only willing to lose less than 1% of their account per trade. For instance, if you have a $20000 trading account, and are willing to risk 0.5% of your capital on each trade, your per trade maximum loss will be $100 (.005 * $20000).

Day trading is going to take your time—many hours, actually. A trader is required to study the markets and smell opportunities, which keep ebbing and flowing during trading hours.

The one beginner mistake for most traders is to start big instead of small. Your untrained mind can only catch up on one or two stocks during a trading session. It is easier to divide your attention between one or two stocks, any more than that would overwhelm your beginner's mind.

Stay away from penny stocks. Penny stocks are liquid and there's not that big a chance of making lots of money.

The worst time to make a move is when the price volatility kicks in. An experienced trader understands the price behavior and knows exactly when to make their move. But as a newbie, you might want to study the patterns first and then start making moves.

What are your entry and exit strategies? Will you use market orders or limit orders? A market order is implemented at the best price during execution, whereas a limit order guarantees the price but not the execution.

When you take up trading, ensure that you have no delusions. You don't have to win all the time in order to make a profit, but you should definitely ensure that your wins have big margins and your losses have smallest margins possible and the difference will put you ahead.

Learn to be grounded and rational. You might be tempted by greed or impulsive decisions, but such would only lead to a bad outcome.

What's your strategy? Oh, no, please don't just freewheel. You need to have a strategy for executing your trades and more importantly, you must adhere to that strategy. Whether you make a loss or profit, learn to move on quickly.

Three rules for the day trader:

- **Be flat at the end of the day.** You should liquidate all trading positions before you close the day.

- **End each day with a profit.** Your purpose of trading is to make a profit. Always aim high, but never worry when you close your day with a tiny profit; a profit is better than a loss.

- **Keep your losses small.** A big loss might harm days of hard work. Your priority is to always win. And if you must lose, it should be in a small margin.

Chapter 17:

Online Trading and Other Emerging Trends

Due to technology advancement, online trading has emerged to be popular among investors. There is software that tracks market performance and places trades and does pretty much everything.

The first thing you must do before trading stocks online is selecting an online broker. Your online broker will perform your trades and keep your money and stock in a secure online account.

There have been many mergers and acquisitions in the world of online trading, but still, there are many independent online firms to select from.

Different firms have diverse levels of assistance, types of accounts, platforms and other services. Before you start trading stocks online, here are some of the important things to keep in mind:

How much money do you have? Does your budget fit in with the requirements of your broker? Some firms will state the minimum deposit required and you must check to be sure that you comply.

How frequently will you trade? Are you going to purchase one type of stock and hold onto it dearly or are you going to be trading on the regular? If you are the kind that rarely trades, you might want to confirm that your broker doesn't charge your account for inactivity. And if you are a regular trader, you might not want a broker that charges small fees per trade.

How experienced are you? Is this your first time doing this? Some brokers offer extensive guides to make you understand every aspect of online trading, but still, that doesn't make up for your lack of experience.

A tech website like Market Watch reviews the performance of brokerages based on rates of success, customer service quality, trading tools and other related factors.

Your broker will require your sensitive information, so make sure that the site is secure with SSL encryption and automatic logouts. Before you pick up a broker, try to read up on their online reviews to get what others are saying about them. A broker who receives tons of negative reviews is obviously problematic.

When you open an account with an online brokerage, you're required to answer a few questions about your financial and investment history.

The brokerage will determine which account is suitable for you. You will provide your social security number, telephone number, and address, in order to put your tax records in order.

You must then select your type of account: individual, joint, custodial or retirement.

Then you must choose between a cash account and a margin account.

Using a cash account, you have to have enough cash to buy stock, but with a margin account, you may have access to credit facilities based on the size of your stock equity.

Also, you must decide how the brokerage will keep your money from trade to trade. Many brokerages provide accounts with the capacity to earn interest, and you get to earn interest from your "idle" money.

Finally, you must fund your account in order to start trading. You can fund your account using wire transfer or any of the popular online payment methods.

When the brokerage activates your account, now you are set to trade.

Chapter 18:

Asset Valuation Principles & Portfolio Management

Asset valuation is the process of finding the worth of a company or any other valuable item. A big part of it involves measuring the assets that produce cash flow.

The advantages of getting an asset valuation include:

- **Having good knowledge of your assets.** An accurate asset valuation helps you understand what your assets are worth. This frees you to make bold investment choices.

- **Preparing for unforeseen investment opportunities.** Having an asset valuation prepares you for unforeseen investment opportunities where you'd ordinarily fail to give the accurate figure. In this way, asset valuation gives you more business.

- **Giving you more power.** Knowing the value of your assets helps you have a strong standing when negotiating a sale.

- **Evaluating the impact.** Having an asset valuation helps you weigh the impact that your assets have on your net worth.

- **Working out the returns.** Having an asset valuation helps an owner work out and compare the returns acquired from their assets.

Asset valuation is mainly carried out before the selling or buying of an asset or before buying insurance for an asset.

Some of the basis of asset valuation is transaction value, cash flows, and other valuation metrics.

Assets consist of securities and commodities, all of which have value. The measurements of working out asset value are both subjective and objective. For instance, it is difficult to quantify the worth of a company's brand by just looking at its financial statements because the brand is an intangible thing and thus valuation is subjective.

On the other hand, net income is an objective measure. If a company intends to acquire another company then its financial statements may be assessed and value known.

Analysts look at both book value and market value of assets. The book value is normally lower than the market value. The commonest way of asset valuation is connected to future cash flows.

Business valuation models:

- Asset-based model

- Earning value model

- Market value model

Asset-based model

It can be arrived at by subtracting total liabilities from the net value of assets or by working out the total amount acquired through liquidation of assets.

Earning value model

This model is based on the concept that the value of the company lies in its ability to generate future wealth. The most common model is through past earning capitalizing.

In this model, what an analyst basically does is to determine the future cash flow of a company by studying the past earnings of the company and multiplying its standardized cash flows by a capitalization factor.

The capitalization factor merely represents the rate of returns a buyer would expect from the investment.

Another formula of earning model is the discounted future earnings. In this model, rather than finding an average of past earnings, an average of projected future earnings is divided by the capitalization factor.

Market value model

In this model, a company is valued by comparing it to similar companies that lately sold. This method can be effective only if there are enough similar companies to act as a benchmark.

Part 5: Critical investment lessons

Chapter 19:

Can you survive on Wall Street?

Wall Street is not a random place on the map where you'd decide to just pack up your stuff and relocate. It is the financial market capital of the US, and by extension, the world.

Firms in Wall Street receive floods of resumes on a daily basis from people who hope to work in Wall Street, but guess what? 98% of all these job seekers get rejected as worthless.

In order to be considered, you will have to stand out. But before you get someone who's willing to even give you the chance to be heard, be prepared to send a ton of emails. With persistence and a bit of luck, you may land an interview and be on the way to working on Wall Street, where you'll be expected to prove yourself over and over again.

You might have heard of people that did courses like anthropology and literature in college, but went on to do great things on Wall Street. Well, such people are not in abundance. Most successful Wall Street figures have a degree in fields like math, finance, accounting, marketing, and economics.

You must target a number of firms and start reaching out to these firms either by phone, post, or email. The rejection rates are very high; don't let it bog you down, just shake it off and move on.

If you get a job in Wall Street, count yourself among the lucky few. But you may have gotten the job, but surviving there is an entirely different matter. If you turn out to be the lazy type, a cheat, a druggie, or exhibit some other vile behaviors, you will be given the boot.

Here are some tips that should help you succeed on Wall Street:

- **Resiliency.** Both physically and mentally. The investment world is a stress-laden industry. There's a small margin of people who survive on Wall Street as the majority are driven out of the place by market forces.

- **Adaptability.** Things move at a rapid pace; there's no stopping. You'll hardly be doing the same thing that you were doing a year or two ago. The people change constantly, the markets shift, new opportunities come up, and in order to adjust to this kind of life, you have got to be adaptable, but with adaptability comes the need of being competent, and so you must ensure that you keep expanding your knowledge in order to qualify for the upgrades that might come your way from time to time.

- **Network.** Wall Street may admittedly be an awful place to make friends because money outs the beast inside every one of us. But at the same time, you must keep the effort to be in "speaking terms" with most people. If you put some effort into networking, you will have access to more deals and you will find yourself with so much work to do. Wall Street can be a cruel place and a lot of people quit and move elsewhere after a taste of what it's like.

- **Ruthless**. It may not be an admirable trait in a person, but in Wall Street, everyone is fighting their own war, and so you must keep your interests as the main priority. Never agree to be short-changed. Also, be economic with your kindness. As the star of Wall Street, Gordon Gekko said, "If you want a friend, get a dog."

Chapter 20: Top 20 Best-Performing Companies

The purpose of going public for every company is to acquire more funds for their operations and expansion. But the aim of an investor is to make a profit. Investors buy stock with the expectation that the share price will go up and thus they will be at a point of selling their shares for a profit. There are many companies who have gone public and went ahead to lose investors' money, while there are other companies who have done exceedingly well. Here is a look at the 20 best-performing companies:

1. ExxonMobil

This is an energy behemoth company. Studies show that the company has generated in excess of one trillion dollars since 1926. Shareholders of ExxonMobil are a happy lot since the company pays dividends handsomely.

2. Apple

The company is synonymous with its moods and unpredictable co-founder, the late Steve Jobs. Apple is still the leader in tech markets under Tim Cook, and besides that, the company has the second best performing stock, with a market capitalization of close to one trillion dollars!

3. Microsoft

Bill Gates dropped out of university to find this company together with his friend Paul Allen. Their first product went on sale in 1985. The following year, the company went public and, as they say, the rest was history. Microsoft stocks have pulled a staggering $629 billion.

4. General Electric

The industrial conglomerate may not be performing exceptionally well at present, considering that even Warren Buffett sold his shares in 2017, but it has a storied history on the stock market. GE was one of the few companies to feature in the original Dow Jones industrial average. Its stock has garnered an estimated $608.1 billion.

5. International Business Machine

IBM creates computer software and hardware. It is one of the longstanding tech companies and its products are a force to reckon with. It has not only survived in an environment of competition from Google, Microsoft, Amazon, and Oracle but also rounds up the top five best-performing stocks.

6. Altria

This American company is one of the biggest distributors of cigarettes, tobacco and other related products. Its stocks are some of the best-performing ones and the lifetime wealth creation stands at $470.2 billion.

7. Johnson & Johnson

Johnson & Johnson is a global company with products in health and pharmaceutical industries. Some of the most popular products of the company include Listerine, Tylenol, Johnson's baby oil, and Johnson's baby shampoo.

8. General Motors

General Motors may have suffered a bankruptcy in 2009 but that doesn't wave off the lifetime performance of its stock. GM went on to stage a comeback under a tough and able CEO, but the stock has not performed as bright as the days of yore.

9. Chevron

An energy conglomerate, the shareholders of Chevron are a happy folk considering that they have enjoyed 30 straight years of dividend increment.

10.   Walmart

One of the world's biggest retailers, founded by a frugal man named Sam Walton. Walmart has the tenth best-performing stocks of all time.

11. Alphabet

This is the parent company of Google, and the performance of its stock is showstopping because Alphabet has been around only for so long.

12. Berkshire Hathaway

One of the true legends of the investment world, Warren Buffett bought a textile company in the 50s and used this company (Berkshire Hathaway) as his investment vehicle, acquiring countless businesses.

13. Procter and Gamble

The company has paid out dividends since the late 19th century and its lifetime wealth creation in the stock market stands at \$355 billion.

14. Amazon

Amazon may have started as a simple website in the book niche, but Jeff Bezos has not only overseen its growth into one of the best-performing companies but also, he's become the world's richest man in the process.

15. Coca-Cola

Coca-cola is almost like the Catholic Church; it has established a presence throughout the world. Its stocks are the 15th best performing of all time.

16. DuPont

It was founded in 1802 as a gunpowder mill by a French-American chemist. This chemical conglomerate has shown consistent performance in the stocks through time and has generated a wealth of about $308 billion.

17. AT & T Corp.

This is an American communication company that provides voice, video, and data services.

18. Merck

This pharmaceutical company was established in 1891 and had displayed consistent performance except in recent years the performance has relatively gone down.

19. Wells Fargo & Co.

Founded in 1852, Wells Fargo has been in the banking industry for quite a long time. The largest shareholder of Wells Fargo is Berkshire Hathaway, with a 10% stake.

20.   Intel

A technology company renowned for making high-quality computer chips, Intel rounds up the top twenty best-performing companies in the stock market.

Chapter 21:
The Power of Diversification

Diversification is the investor's main defense against risk. An investor commits their resources to a wide range of investment categories. Diversification's main role may be to spread risk, but just as important is the ability to generate revenue.

Most investment professionals have said that diversification may not protect you 100% from loss, but it is a sure method of wealth creation and a dependable formula of attaining future financial goals while keeping risk at the minimum.

These are the two types of risks that investors face:

Undiversifiable. It is also referred to as "systematic risk," and it touches every company. The common risks in this category include high inflation rate, high exchange rate, political chaos, war, and high interest rates. This type of risk is beyond your control and there's no escape.

Diversifiable; also known as "unsystematic risk," it is category specific. This risk only touches certain companies, industries, markets, economies, and countries. This kind of risk can be effectively watered down through diversification. The unsystematic risk may be triggered by market forces or by poor investment decisions. Business risk and financial risk make up the most of unsystematic risk.

Case in point:

Let's say you have a portfolio investment of only Wells Fargo. When a major scandal rocks the company or when there is major market turmoil in the banking sector, their share price will tumble down. Your investment portfolio will lose significant value.

However, had you diversified your portfolio so that you had invested in securities in other economic sectors like airlines and railways and water companies, your investment portfolio would have absorbed the loss originating from the Wells Fargo deal.

Also, it is important that you diversify in different asset classes. For instance, bonds and stocks never give a similar reaction to unfavorable market conditions.

Diversification helps the market go up, thus improving index funds. When businesses have more resources, they may devote these resources to service delivery improvement and research and development of products. The world of investing embodies the idea of "one hand washing the other," and so businesses cannot make huge profits unless they have huge resources to optimize their products.

Diversification helps assess your performance. An investor who considers himself great needs to have proof of that. What better than to have a diverse portfolio? Having a diverse portfolio will help you make a judgment on your investment decisions. If a certain investment consistently shows great results while other investment consistently brings up poor results, you might want to sell off the poor investment and commit more resources to the investment that is doing well. This environment gives you a better idea of what works, and you can gauge your ability to select performing investments.

Regulatory and legislative risks. There are some risks which exist outside of the markets, for instance, regulations and legislation. Some jurisdictions might come up with oppressive legislation or the governing bodies might develop new rules. If the rules have any adverse effects your portfolio would be a sort of cushion against the negative impact.

Investment diversification is the secret to fast-tracking wealth creation. Warren Buffett may not have become the greatest all-time investor if he'd chosen to focus on developing the textile company he'd acquired in the 50s.

Chapter 22:

Role of Technology in Trading & Profit Growth

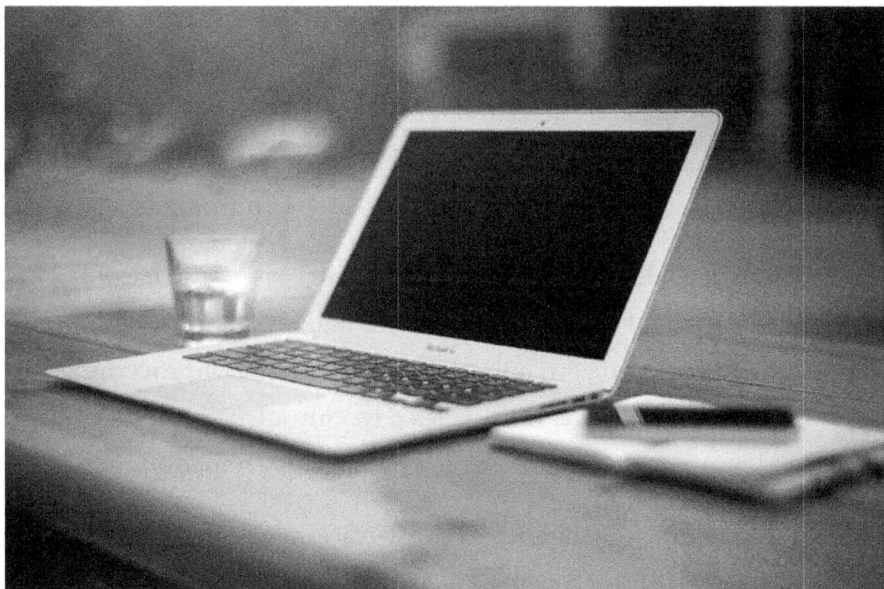

Technology has disrupted many sectors and the investment world is no exception. Even staunch anti-technology investors like Warren Buffett seem to have softened their stance on technology with his recent buying of Apple shares. It sends a message, technology is the future, and you either adapt or get thrown out.

Technology has helped companies evolve from targeting local markets into focusing on even an international consumer base. In many sectors, technology has improved on product creation and service delivery.

In the financial markets, the biggest role that technology plays is in data processing, storage, and other related services. The result of utilizing technology in financial markets has been high profits, smooth operations, and high client retention. Technology, it seems, is an aid to finance professionals, and not a threat as the uneducated person might want you to think.

Asset management has been a hands-on activity where fund managers select investments that they figure will generate the most profit for their clients. The dynamics of picking up the securities with the greatest potential are exhaustive. So, actively managing funds is a very resource-intensive undertaking, but what about passive fund's?

Passive funds differ from actively managed funds in the sense that the manager isn't very hands-on. An example of passive funds investment is index funds and exchange-traded-funds (ETFs).

The interesting thing is that investors are slowly ditching actively-managed funds and moving to passive funds. One of the obvious reasons is that passive funds attract significant administrative fees, but also, passive funds have a big room for technology optimization.

According to a research by PWC, passive investments will make up 35% of the asset management sector by 2020, chiefly because investors will seek low-fee investments and a large market exposure. And this development will affect the traditional asset managers who ask for high fees even though the investments of their clients are not always profitable.

Obviously, passive investments appeal to investors because of the added advantage of technological optimization.

There are existing technologies that manage investment funds automatically, placing trades and seeking maximum exposure all on autopilot. Normally, these technologies are software that you have to pay annual fees to obtain a license. Is the software accurate? It seems so, because there many online traders nowadays making a hell lot of money from automated trading.

The reason why traditional asset managers charge their clients a lot of money is simply because there's a lot of background work that goes toward making an investment profitable. Asset managers charge high fees because they pay researchers and analysts before reaching their decision and also they require adequate compensation for purposes of underscoring trust. However, automated program take the roles of researching, analyzing, detecting bad deals, placing trades, almost everything that an asset manager does, except that the robot advisor charges very low fees (annual software license fees).

As more advances are being made in the artificial intelligence sector, it is expected that powerful trading robots will be created, which can even outdo professional investors.

In such a scenario, the difference between making a loss and profit would not be chalked to humans, but the type of robot employed. But one thing is sure: robots will complement finance professionals rather than eliminate them.

Chapter 23:

The Role of a Stockbroker

A stock broker merely acts on the wishes of the investor. A stockbroker will connect a buyer to a seller and thus create liquidity. The work of a stockbroker is tough and it involves advising their clients on investment moves that will guarantee them high returns. A stock broker's activity for the day include researching, meeting clients, and being present on the floor for the trade executions. A broker's salary is in the form of commissions, and so his income might be quite unsteady.

A stock broker needs to have the right background in university and should have a degree related to these fields: business, economics, finance, and math. Also, they should have an extensive knowledge of the free markets and especially securities investments, as this is where most of their clients want to invest.

A stockbroker takes care of the needs of the investor. The following are the benchmarks for identifying a good stock broker:

- Experienced in public funds investing

- Skilled in competitive pricing

- Independent thinker

- Knowledge of the market

- Ability to make tactical and well-considered ideas

- Ability and willingness to inform you on important trends

- Owns important analytical tools

- Skilled at analyzing credit

- Skilled at economic research

- Skilled at income research

- Good execution of trades

The life of a stockbroker is hectic, and for good reason, they carry the hopes of many investors. Stockbrokers have great influence on the decisions of investors. Here are some of the roles of stockbrokers:

Contacting prospective clients. A stockbroker needs to have a client list, it doesn't matter whether they work individually or whether they work for a trading firm. So, they must put the effort in adding new clients to their list, following up on deals with current clients, and maintaining relationships with other industry professionals. Ideally, a successful stockbroker has an extensive network.

Trade executions. It is the duty of the stockbroker to buy or sell on behalf of their client. Nowadays, the stockbroker may buy or sell with just a push of the button on their computer, but in the days of yore, it was through phone calls or person to person.

Fair dealing. A stockbroker has a lot of information in his head. He could decide to use this information for illegal practices by luring naïve and unsuspecting investors. However, the regulatory authorities require that a stockbroker handles their client with transparency and in as fair a manner as possible. Stock brokers should not hold back critical information, especially when it's the kind that could influence the investor's decision.

Loyalty. A stockbroker earns through commissions. Sometimes, greed may come into the scene, leading to a clash between the interests of the stockbroker and those of their client. However, a stockbroker should at all time focus on the interests of their client first.

Supervision. A stockbroker has the duty of supervising their client's resources. This involves tracking developing trends and warning their client in case of an impending calamity. Stockbrokers have a great deal of information on their hands, and one thing hasn't said or one thing said makes a world of difference.

Chapter 24:
The Legends of the Stock Market

A great investor is a good master of money. The father of value investing, Ben Graham, is credited as inspiring modern investors and giving them the wisdom of investing intelligently. A successful investor is appreciated in the financial world, where success is mostly a result of hard work and a lucky break. These are the most successful investors of all time.

1. Warren Buffett

The Oracle of Omaha is the faithful disciple of Ben Graham and he proudly says so. He's managed to accumulate a net worth of $81 billion through his investment vehicle, Berkshire Hathaway. Warren Buffett started investing at the age of 11 but it wasn't until his fifties that he made his first billion.

2. George Soros

Born in Hungary, George Soros migrated to England and then to America where he made his fortune. George had started out working on the railway and in a hotel before he made the shift to the financial markets. His first job in finance was in a company named Singer & Friedlander in London.

3. Prince Alwaleed Bin Talal Alsaud

A Saudi royal, Prince Alwaleed owns equities in multinational companies through his investment companies. In 2008, the prince was listed as one of the most influential people by Time's Magazine.

4. Carl Icahn

Carl Icahn began his financial career in Wall Street as a stockbroker. He'd later form his own securities firm and start buying stocks of companies. Some of the companies where he holds majority stocks include: RJR, Texaco,

Nabisco, Gulf & Western, American Can, USX, Revlon, Marvel Comics and Fairmont Hotels

5. Alisher Burkhanovich Usmanov

The richest man in Russia also happens to be an investor. Alisher Burkhanovch Usmanov has a big interest in the metal works and energy industry. Through his investment vehicle, he has purchased shares in wide-ranging sectors.

6. Ronald Perelman

Ronald is famously known as a corporate raider of the 80s, but he made his fortune through purchasing majority shares of big companies. He's the owner of AM General, the manufacturer of military crafts like the Humvee. His other investments touch upon many sectors like banks, entertainment, security, gaming, apparels, cosmetics, and publishing.

7. Mikhail Prokhorov

He's big on sports, particularly basketball, but Mikhail made his fortune by investing in the metals and mining sectors. He owns the investment company ONEXIM Group, with assets valued at $17 billion.

8. David Tepper

David Tepper was an investment banker working for Goldman Sachs before he quit and started his own fund, Appaloosa Management. He attracted many clients and made great investment decisions which saw high returns. His success secret was "Investing in the diciest of companies."

9. Philip Anschutz

Philip is definitely big on sports. He owns both Los Angeles Lakers and Los Angeles Kings and also played a huge part in starting Major League Soccer. He started in the oil business, but branched out into the railway industry, and now his investment claws have reached a wide range of sectors.

10. Stephen Schwarzman

Stephen Schwarzman started out as a banker at Lehman Brothers and was promoted to the position of managing director in a short length of time. In 1985, Stephen and his friends started the Blackstone Group, a company dedicated to acquisitions. Then the company got into leveraged buyouts of companies drawn from a wide range of industries.

Chapter 25:

Types of Securities

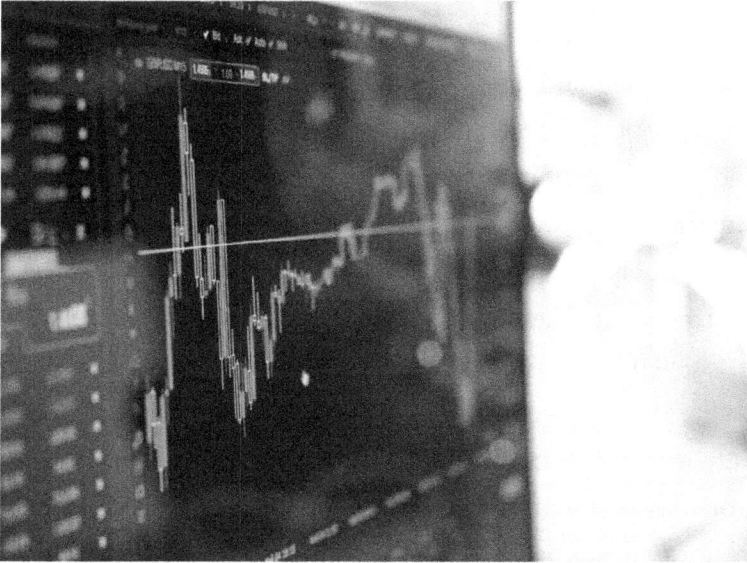

Securities are financial instruments that have value. They may be represented in part or the majority ownership of public companies, credit against governments, or any other ownership rights.

Shares. A share represents an equity security. The holder of shares has ownership of part or majority of the company that issued the shares. Thus, the holder of shares has the right of making contributions, whether intelligent or otherwise that affect the management of the company. In other words, a shareholder has a say. Investors buy shares with the intention of earning returns known as dividends. When a company earns a profit, part of the profit is distributed to shareholders as dividends. The number of dividends paid out is decided by the shareholders and the board.

Bonds. A bond represents a debt security. When you purchase a bond, you may have no say in the company, but are entitled to receive an interest for a fixed period of time, and when your bond matures, you may receive your principal back. Also, the company may get you to agree to regular annual payments of the principal. The issuer usually pays interest once or twice per year.

Open-end funds. An open-end fund represents a diversified portfolio of securities investments. The securities investments are carefully selected and managed by a fund management company. The fund does not have fixed capital and thus investors are the primary source of funds. Open-end funds may invest in local or international markets in all manner of securities. The fund manager determines the overall investment strategy. Open-end funds, are not normally traded on exchanges, and indeed there are very few exchanges where shares of open-end funds may be bought across the world. Open-end funds are normally purchased through fund management companies. But you may buy shares of open-end funds through a brokerage firm, and the investor may not pay any other fees but the broker's fees.

Index open-end funds. A fund manager allocates investors' resources into securities investments, thus making up an index. The yield of the index must be tracked.

Before units of index open-end funds are purchased, a declaration of accession must be signed. Afterward, assets are moved into a special account open at a bank. The fund management company will charge appropriate fees upon buy or sell executions. Investors are charged a fee by management and also pay for custodial services. The shares of open-end funds are bought and sold at net asset value, as calculated by the fund management company. Minor investors may buy index open-end funds at the market rate and are not charged entry or exit fees.

Closed-end funds; A closed-end fund involves investing resources into securities of other issuers. The management company gets to decide which securities to include in its portfolio.

Investment certificates. These are debt securities issued by a bank that offers an investor a set amount of money. But there are conditions. The issuers of investment certificates are mainly banks, and before you invest in investment certificate you might want to first check the credit rating of a bank.

Warrants. These are options offered by a joint-stock company that gives investors the right to buy a certain amount of the company's shares at a set price.

Chapter 26:

Rule #1: Never Lose Money!

You have probably heard of this quote by Warren Buffett, *"Rule No. 1: Never lose money. Rule No. 2: Don't forget rule No. 1."*

One of the biggest challenges for an investor is keeping their head level in the midst of chaos. A stock market is a chaotic place, no doubt.

For instance, a new company may go public and people will buy shares and be hopeful that the company will become a huge market player, except the company turns out to be a huge flop with zero public interest and no prospects of ever doing great business. So when investors see that, their base reaction is disappointment, yes. They get disappointed because this is yet another company threatening to lose their money.

Most investors rush to sell their stocks and at least break even or make a small loss. But what is the intelligent investor supposed to do? They are supposed to do their homework and evaluate the chances of survival of this company in the long run. The biggest companies never started off with a hoot after all.

As an investor, it is very hard not to lose money if you have not mastered your emotions. Actually, if you look at investments through the prism of emotions, that makes you a speculator, not an investor, and you set yourself up for failure.

When you commit your resources to an investment, there are many hazards to be fought. The biggest of all is risky. You risk losing part or whole of your money.

But Warren Buffett says that risk can be eliminated, or at least can be brought to the minimum. You eliminate risk by being competent at what you are doing. When you know what you are doing, it won't be a stab in the dark anymore, but rather a sure bet.

The best way to become competent at what you are doing is through extensive research. It's amazing how lazy investors could get. When they come across a "promising investment" they just do a quick Google search to determine the parties involved, stalk their Facebook to see what they look like or how hilarious they are, and then they speed dial their broker to make the purchase.

Due diligence and fundamental analysis might not be very pleasurable activities, but they make up investment safety 101. An intelligent investor is his own best protector: he's more anxious about not losing money than he is about seeing a return.

Amidst all these, what is the place of gut feeling?

We often hear successful people tell us that they trusted their guts when it was time to make this big decision. But should investors also trust their guts where the viability of an investment is concerned?

Yes, they should do it and then back it up with fundamental analysis. In that sense, the spirit of fundamental analysis is to solidify your interest, rather than look for holes. However, if you come across red flags, then it's time to be rational and ignore your gut feeling.

After all, if you step back from an investment, it doesn't mean you lost, it means you still have the resources to invest in another project.

Never lose money.

Chapter 27:

Avoid These Mistakes that Even Smart Investors Make

An intelligent investor learns from the mistakes of others because the investment world can be unforgiving. Most of the time, the mistakes that ruin you are big mistakes, but they start small. These are some of the mistakes to keep guard against:

Having no plan. An investor should have a sense of direction. Having a plan alleviates anxiety and puts you in a place of power. You know what you are looking for. Your plan should address the following:

- **Goals and objectives.** Instead of having vague goals like, "I want to get rich doing this," say instead, "I want to make $100000 this year from the stock market."

- **Risks.** As an investor, you are going to have to make peace with risk. It will always be there. Thank goodness, because risk does a good job of chewing up incompetent investors. So, be aware of the risks that your investments might run into and either minimize them or be prepared to lose.

- **Measure.** Have a system in place to measure the effectiveness of your investment strategies.

Failing to diversify. But you must take care to diversify in the best-performing assets, otherwise you risk compounding failure and ending up in a much worse state. You also need to diversify across different asset classes. Diversification is the surest method of protecting yourself against major risk.

Investing in a short scale of time. Long-term investing is the mark of a true investor. However, most people seem to want to commit their resources to an investment only for so long, maybe its anxiety or life pressures, but they liquidate their securities very soon and move on to something else, thus killing off the momentum of their profits.

Wasting time on TV. Most of the news on TV is negative and it's deliberately so. Thought you'd find great investment wisdom on TV? Nope!

You cannot get worthy investment advice for free. You will have to subscribe to an authority (which costs money) or buy books or other related media.

Manager worship. Some people seem to think that the success of their investments is hinged upon the fund manager. It's true. Managers will select the securities, investment that their fund will invest in. In that sense, they play a big part in realizing success. However, when an investor becomes obsessed about who's running the fund, they have lost it. The important thing is that they are competent.

Timing the market. There is no such thing as timing the market. You only get burned trying to do that. If you have the resources, you just go into it and implement your strategy, focusing on portfolio diversification.

Neglecting your investments. Investments may be passive activity, but it doesn't mean that it's one-strike affair. You need to check your investments regularly and rebalance your assets in order to stay aligned with your goals.

Not researching. If you haven't got the facts, you are susceptible to failure. Research makes up a big part of knowing what you are getting yourself into and thus arming yourself against risk.

When failure to research becomes a habit, it might cost you your investment career along with your resources, become another loser, and fellow investors will be looking at you and shaking their heads.

Chapter 28:
Glossary of Stock Market Terms

Agent: a securities firm that acts on behalf of its clients as a seller or buyer of a security.

Annual report: a publication that includes financial statements and operations report.

Arbitrage: the simultaneous buying of a security on one stock market and selling on another stock market in order to make a profit.

Assets: the valuable resources of a company or person such as securities, money, real estate, and equipment.

Bear market: When stock prices of a market fall down.

Bid: the highest price that a buyer is willing to pay for a stock.

Bonds: these are the promissory notes given by a public corporation or government to the lenders usually with a fixed amount within a fixed length of time.

Broker or brokerage firm: this is a securities firm or a registered financial advisor affiliated with a firm.

Bull market: where the stock prices are rising.

Capital: fixed assets, securities and other financial assets of an investor.

Capital gain or loss: the profit or loss after selling assets that are classified under income tax as capital assets.

Certificate: the physical document that indicates ownership of a stock, bond, and other security.

Closed-end investment fund: an investment trust that offers a set number of securities that trade on a stock exchange or in the over-the-counter market.

Commission: the fees that a broker requires for buying or selling securities on behalf of the investor.

Commodities: commerce products traded on an authorized commodities exchange.

Common shares: securities that represent a fraction of ownership in a company and generally bestow voting rights.

Daily price limit: the utmost price advance or dip for a futures contract in a trading session compared to the settlement price of the day before.

Day order: this is an order that is applicable only for the day it was entered.

Diversification: an investment style of minimizing risk whereby an investor purchases different types of securities.

Equities: stocks that represent a share in company ownership.

Underwriting: the purchase of securities for resale.

Venture capital: money raised by firms to finance business projects.

Warrant: a security that gives the holder the right to buy securities at a set price.

Yield: shown as a percentage, this is the measure of the return on an investment.

Conclusion

As Warren Buffett aptly put it, *"Rule No. 1: Don't lose money."*

The best way an investor may guard himself against losing money is by ensuring that they invest in securities where they are sure to win. Is that even possible? Yes. When you are competent at what you're doing, the element of risk is greatly minimized—eliminated, even. So the challenge is to become competent at what you're doing.

Every investor is helpless against "unsystematic risk." This is the risk that humans have no control over. It may visit upon investors in the form of inflation, market failure, political instability or an unfavorable legislation.

The best way to cover yourself against the cruel hands of risk is by spreading your portfolio. When you allocate your resources in different asset classes, you spread the risk, and thus you are less likely to be held back by the loss.

Fundamental analysis is important. Listening to your gut is not a bad thing. However, you should also evaluate a company's financial health before committing your resources to the company.

The main benefit of fundamental analysis is that it gives you a chance to find out whether a company is undervalued. An undervalued stock hasn't reached its intrinsic value. And so, buying an undervalued stock is a great investment decision, in the sense that when the prices go up you stand to gain a huge profit.

The worst trait in an investor is emotional instability. This kind of investor responds to negative market trends with fear-based actions.

The biggest quality in an investor is rationality.

Options Trading

How to Make Money in Less Than 7 Days

Table of Contents

Introduction

Congratulations on downloading this book and thank you for doing so.

The following chapters will teach you the ins and outs of options trading:

Chapter 1 talks about the basics so that you will have a good foundation and understanding of what options trading is really all about.

Chapter 2 discusses the risks and benefits of options trading.

Chapter 3 teaches powerful and effective strategies that you can use to increase your chances of making the right trading decisions.

Chapter 4 reveals the important keys to success to help make you a better options trader.

Chapter 5 lays down the common mistakes that you should avoid.

Chapter 6 discusses the successful trader's mindset. It is the right mindset if you want to make continuous profits with options trading.

May this book be your guide to success, happiness, and financial freedom

There are plenty of books on this subject on the market, thanks again for choosing this one! Every effort was made to ensure it is full of as much useful information as possible. Please enjoy!

Chapter 1: Options Trading 101

What is options trading?

Options trading is also called *binary options*. It is like trading stocks and forex. However, you do not have to purchase any assets. Instead, you simply have to speculate if the price of a particular asset will increase or decrease at expiry date. Many traders get attracted to options trading due to its simplicity. It is also worth noting that this kind of trading has a fixed risk as well as a fixed payout.

Options trading vs. gambling

There are people who confuse options trading with gambling. In fact, in some jurisdictions, trading options is already considered as gambling. Just like a game of roulette where you can wager if the ball will land on red or black, in options trading, you simply have to speculate if the price of an underlying asset will rise or fall at a specified time. Also, just like many gambling games, there is a fixed payout if you are able to predict the outcome correctly.

Does this mean that options trading is gambling? Well, it depends on how you approach it. If you trade options by relying on mere guesswork, then you can consider that to be gambling. But if every "wager" that you make is backed up with a thorough research and a good understanding of the asset concerned, and if you consider every decision as an investment decision, then you are trading/investing and not just gambling. Take note that this does not necessarily mean that gambling is completely bad, especially once you witness how the casino sharks dominate a table. However, it is not advisable to approach options trading as a mere gamble, because doing so can significantly increase the chances of losing all your investment. Now, whether you view options trading as gambling or not is a free choice that you can make. The important thing here is the profit that you have earned if any.

Options trading vs. forex and stock trading

When you trade options, you do not have to buy currencies or stocks. You do not get to own any assets. Instead, you merely speculate if the price of a particular asset will rise or fall at expiry date. Another distinct difference is that when you trade options, there is a fixed payout. You will know how much you will earn if you make the right decisions. When you trade forex or stocks, there is no fixed profit potential. You cannot tell the exact profit that you can earn. Also, when you trade currencies or stocks, you will normally have to wait for long weeks and months just to earn a significant amount of profit. When you trade options, you can earn even as high as 1,000% of your investment quickly, even in as fast as a few minutes. Of course, this is not that easy to do, but it is possible as long as you can speculate the price movements correctly. When you trade options, there are fewer fees for you to worry about. There is no need for you to be concerned of any surcharges, volume restrictions, and others. Last but not least, it is much easier to learn trading options than forex or stock trading.

Is it for you?

So, is options trading for you? It is true that almost anyone can start trading options right away, but not everyone can achieve success with options trading. To increase your chances of making continuous profits, you should put in enough time and efforts. If you are not willing to do serious research and analysis, then perhaps options trading is not for you. It is not uncommon for professional options traders spend long hours in research and analysis. You simply cannot rely on mere guesswork. You have to study the market and the assets that you are dealing with. Whether options trading is for you or not is something that only you can decide. The good news is that it is something that you can learn. Even if you think that you do not have what it takes to be a successful options trader at the present time, you can still make adjustments and learn to be a great options trader.

Assets

Options trading is about speculating the price movement of a particular asset. You should predict if its price will rise higher or fall lower than its current price at expiry date. What are assets? Assets are usually defined as "financial instruments that have value." When you trade options, there are different assets that you can work on, such as stocks, commodities, and currency pairs, among others.

Call/Put

When you trade options, you just have to choose between two decisions: call or put. You should choose to *call* if you speculate that the price of the asset will be higher than its current price at expiry time, and you should choose the *put* option if you think that the value of an asset will be lower than its current price at expiry time.

Take note that some trading platforms use other terms for these. You may encounter terms like up and down, above and below, high and low, rise and fall, and others. However, they all refer to the same choices that you have when you trade options: call vs. put.

Strike price

For a Call option, the strike price represents the price at which the asset can be bought at a specified time. For a Put option, the strike price signifies the price at which an underlying asset may be sold.

Expiry date

The expiry date simply refers to the end of a trading period. This is the time when you will know if you have made the right (or wrong) trading decision. When you trade options, you can choose the time frame just how long you want it to last. You can choose an expiry date that is a long way from now, but you can also choose a trading period that is as fast as a few minutes or even as quick as 60 seconds. In choosing the right expiry date for you, you should consider the kind of strategy that you are using. For example, technical analysis is an excellent strategy for trades that have a short timeframe. Do not worry; we will tackle this strategy later in the book. For now, just read and focus on learning the basics.

Long-term option vs. Speed option

As the name implies, a long-term option is one that lasts for a long period of time. However, the word "long" is relative. In options trading, long-term options are options are last for at least 24 hours or longer. Speed option is the kind of option that has a shorter period. It can take just a few hours, but it can also be as fast as a minute or so. This is as close as you can get to casino gambling.

In-the-money vs. Out-the-money

In-the-money refers to a winning trade. Hence, it means profit. It signifies that you have made the right decision and won a trade. On the contrary, out-the-money means that you just lost a trade.

Bear market vs. Bull market

These two terms describe the status of the market. When you say that it is a bear market, it means that the prices of assets are falling or are just about to decrease. When you say that the market is a bull market, it means that the prices of certain assets are increasing or are about to increase. Now, unlike trade stocks or currencies, you can still earn money from options trading even in the case of a bear market. This is because your profits do not rely on the prices of assets, but if you are able to predict or speculate their price movements. This is one of the best reasons to trade options. You can still make a substantial amount of profits regardless of the situation of assets in the market.

What to look for in an options trading broker

Before you can start trading options, you first need to open an account with a broker. When you make a search online, you will find a long list of brokers that seem to offer the same service. So, how do you know which one will best suit your needs? Here are the set standards to look for:

- Trading platform

It should be noted that it is your broker that will provide you with the platform that you can use for options trading. As a rule, it should make the experience of trading more convenient and fun for you. The platform should be easy to use. Although the design of the platform is not considered very important by some traders, it is still a good idea to pick a platform that is professionally designed as it can help to put you in the right mood for trading. The platform should also provide you with free tools, such as graphs, to help you come up with the best trading decision.

- Customer support

It is extremely important that you work with a broker that has an active and reliable customer support team. The support team can be helpful, especially if you encounter technical problems or if you simply have any inquiry regarding the trading platform. A broker will give you some ways to reach the support team. Normally, the customer support can be contacted via email, or via on-page chat. There might also be a number that you can call. Make sure that you take note of the way/ways that your broker provides to contact the support team.

- Mobile feature

These days, it is much easier to access the Internet on your mobile device, and brokers are well aware of this. This is why most, if not all, of the top brokers out there offer a mobile feature of the trading platform. This will allow you to engage in options trading at any time by simply using your mobile phone. Normally, you will not be able to use all the features of the trading platform if you use the mobile feature, but it should allow you to use the important parts of the platform, such as being able to place your trade, make deposits and a withdrawal, and others.

- Demo account

Your broker should provide you with a demo account. The demo account will allow you to make trades in a real options trading environment without risking anything. It is also a good tool to use when testing out your strategy. If you are just starting out, then you are encouraged to practice with the demo account until you become familiar with the actual practice of options trading.

- Positive reviews

Before you make a deposit into your trading account, you should first check the reviews given to your broker. This is easy to do: Simply use your favorite browser, type the name of the broker, add the word "reviews," and then press the *enter* key. The search engine results page (SERP) will then show you relevant pages. Make sure that your broker has positive reviews. Also, pay attention to the dates when the reviews were made. You want to read the latest reviews. It is okay if a broker has some negative reviews as long as the positive reviews outweigh the negative. It is important that you only work with a reliable broker. Unfortunately, there are many scammers online who only want to rip you off of your money. By checking the latest reviews, you can lower the chances of having to deal with an unreliable broker.

- Availability of assets

It is good if your broker has a wide selection of assets. Although this is not required as you can always make a profit despite the status of the market. In options trading, the only important thing is to make the right speculations. Even if the price of an asset drops, you can still make a nice profit. This is one of the reasons why so many people these days want to learn about options trading. There is always the opportunity to make a high profit regardless of the current market situation.

- Payout

Different brokers may offer different payouts. Choose a broker that offers a high payout. Ideally, your broker should offer a payout of at least 85%. Some brokers even give a payout as high as 90% or even 95%. Just be sure to work with a trustworthy broker.

- Banking options

Be sure to check the banking options provided by your broker. It is not uncommon for brokers provide more ways to make a deposit, but only limited methods for making a withdrawal. Make sure that the options offered by your broker are available for you for making a deposit and withdrawal. You should also check the requirements that your broker might impose when requesting for a withdrawal. It is common for brokers to ask for copies of certain documents, such as a valid ID and a proof of billing before they even start to process a withdrawal request. Make sure that you have such documents in your possession and that they have not yet expired. If you have more concerns about this matter, kindly contact the customer support team. you want to avoid the situation where you have lots of funds and profits in your account but have no way of withdrawing them.

- Security

Your broker should offer powerful security. Ideally, your broker's site should be encrypted especially every time that you need to input sensitive information like your password. There are many hackers online, so be sure that you also focus on the security of your account. If your broker offers additional security features like a two-factor authenticator where you will have to input a code after your password to access your account, then be sure to make use of them also. Although this might seem a hassle for a beginner, it also helps to ensure the security of your trading account. Also, you will probably have to leave your money in your account, so you really have to use a secure site so that you would not have to worry about losing your funds. Make security a priority. Unfortunately, some traders only realize the importance of having tight security after they have already lost their funds.

By then, it is already too late. Remember that when it comes to the money or funds that you keep online, having a strong security should be a primary priority.

Chapter 2: Risks and Benefits

Risks

- Market risk

Whether you make a profit or not will depend on the price movement of the asset involved, and this price movement depends on how the market behaves. It is difficult to tell the direction that the market will take. This simply depends on so many factors that are outside of your control. Hence, no matter how much research you do, never forget this element of market risk.

- Lack of ownership

When you trade binary options, you do not get to own the stock or commodity that is being traded. You are merely speculating its price movement, whether it is going to rise or fall at expiry time. You do not exercise any form of ownership.

- High risk

Options trading is a high-risk investment. Although you can earn even as high as 90% or even higher in a single trade, there is a risk of losing all of your invested funds in a trade if you make the wrong decision. This means that if, for example, you wager $200, and you lose the trade, then you will lose the whole $200 instantly. This is unlike trading forex or stocks where you still retain ownership over what is left and be able to sell them to at least recover some of your losses. But, do not let this discouraged you as the profit potential in options trading is also very high. As the saying goes, "high risk, high return."

- Not liquid

Options do not have any liquidity. If you enter into a trade, you will have to wait for the trading period to end. In the meantime, you simply have to hope for the best. There are traders who will allow you to cancel a trade, but this is normally exercised only in a short timeframe and can even come with a fee. This is usually used only when you enter a trade by mistake. However, you should also understand that liquidity should not be much of an issue when you trade options since you can choose to trade within a short timeframe only, even as fast as 1 minute.

- Limited potential profit

When you trade options, there is already a predetermined payout even before you enter into a trade. Therefore, you will already know just how much you can earn. Of course, in case you make the wrong trading decision, you will lose all the funds that you invested in a trade. This is unlike investing in stocks or currencies where there is no particular ceiling as to how much you can earn. However, it is also noteworthy that when you invest in stocks, a profit of 25% in a year is already considered high. Since currencies are already well established and are strictly regulated, their prices do not fluctuate significantly. Now, compare this with the around 90% profit potential when you trade options which you can earn in just a few minutes.

- High probability of losing

It is true that many people who invest in options trading lose their money. Although you may encounter stories of people who triple or even multiply their money by more than five times in a few minutes, there are many other stories where they lose all their funds in one trading day. Just as you options trading can make you money quickly, it can also cause you to lose all your funds quickly. This is why you need to understand it and develop an effective strategy.

Benefits

- High return

If you think that a 30% profit is already considered high, wait until you see how much you can earn when you trade options. With options trading, you can earn as high as around 90% in a single trade, which can be as fast as one minute. There are, of course, other time frames that you can use.

- Simple

Options trading is not a complicated process. It is just like predicting the outcome of a coin flip. In this case. You simply have to decide if it is going to be a call or a put. Indeed, you can easily learn how to trade options in just a few minutes.

- A wide range of assets

With binary options, you will have a lot of choices as to where to put an investment. After all, you would not purchase any stock or asset. In fact, some brokers will allow you to trade with a minimum amount of $1. If you use bitcoins, you can even find brokers that will allow you to trade binary options, even with less than a dollar per trade.

- Limited risk

You do not have to worry about risking more than you can afford to lose. There are no surcharges or any other hidden charges for you to worry about. The extent of your risk is limited to the amount of your wager.

- Gambling factor

Gambling is fun. This is why many people get addicted to it. When you deal with options trading there is this gambling factor that you can enjoy.

However, it is noteworthy that you should not allow this gambling impulse to take control of your decisions. If you want to have consistent success with trading binary options, you should take the time and efforts to study the different assets, develop a strategy, and come up with the right trading decisions.

- Quick

When you trade options, there are different timelines that you can choose from. A trade can last for days and weeks, but you can also choose a timeline that is as fast as an hour, five minutes, or even just one minute. Some brokers even offer a timeframe of less than one minute. Hence, if you are interested in making quick trades, then you should definitely look into options trading.

Now that you know the benefits and risks associated with options trading, are you still willing to pursue it? If you take a closer look, you will realize that the benefits completely outweigh the risks involved. After all, in any investment or trade, there are always risks involved. It will just depend on how much risk you are willing to handle. If you are still deciding to pursue options trading, then it is time for you to learn effective strategies that can help pave your way to success.

Chapter 3: Powerful Strategies

When you trade options, you need to apply the right strategies to increase your chances of making the right trading decisions. It is not a good idea to just gamble and rely solely on luck. If you want to have continuous success trading binary options, then you must approach it the right way: by using powerful and effective strategies.

> Fundamental analysis

Fundamental analysis is considered to be the *lifeblood of investment.* It is probably one of the most important strategies that you should use. In fact, expert traders advise that if you are serious about trading options, then you should definitely make use of fundamental analysis.

As the name implies, this strategy deals with the fundamentals or the basics. This is important since it deals with the foundation of the asset involved. Take note, however, that fundamental analysis is not limited to just the asset itself, but also takes into consideration other factors, such as the economy, current market trend, competition, and technological developments, among others. The idea behind this strategy is that by studying and analyzing the fundamentals, you will be more able to come up with the right trading decision. For example, if there is a news piece that states that the employment rate in the U.S. has significantly increased, there is a good chance that the price of USD will increase. This will allow you to make the right options trading decision since you now have an idea of the direction that the USD will take.

Fundamental analysis is not just about the economy. One of the major forces that drive the economy is business. Therefore, you need to take a closer look and study various businesses, as well as how they affect one another. You have to analyze their financial statements, their competitors, and their performance in the market, among others. It is also noteworthy that fundamental analysis can be applied together with another strategy.

Indeed, this approach is probably one that demands the most time and efforts, but it is very much worth it. In fact, it would be rare to find a successful and professional options trader who does not use fundamental analysis on a regular basis. Keep in mind that the more that you understand the basics, the more that you can come up with the right trading decision.

➢ Technical analysis

This strategy makes use of graphs and charts, so if you are more of a visual person, then you will most likely enjoy using this strategy. With technical analysis, you will analyze the performance of an underlying asset to predict its future movement. If you are not fond of analyzing hard facts and numbers, then this strategy is the way to go. The charts and graphs will show you the price movements of the asset concerned over a period of time. The idea behind this approach is that the different factors that can affect an asset has had their final effect on the price. Therefore, by simply dealing directly with the price movements, you also get to deal with all these factors. This makes the work much simpler and more direct. After all, whether you make a profit or not will depend on how the price of an asset moves.

When you use technical analysis, the key is to learn to identify and take advantage of patterns. However, the problem is that patterns come and go. Therefore, just because you have studied a particular graph for an hour does not always mean that there is a pattern for you to see. A common mistake is to force to see a pattern even when it does not really exist. Remember to never create a pattern when it is not there. You need to keep an open and unbiased mind when you examine any graph or chart. Again, it is your broker that should provide you with helpful tools like graphs/charts.

Do patterns really exist? The answer here is *yes*. In fact, even a random generator creates patterns every now and then. Once you spot a pattern, then you will know how an asset will move, and you can use that to your advantage. Just remember to be careful with identifying a pattern since patterns come and go.

Just like fundamental analysis, you can safely apply technical analysis to another strategy. In fact, many expert traders combine fundamental analysis and technical analysis.

➢ Go with the flow

This is a very common strategy used even by those who have not read anything about options trading. So, be careful when you use this strategy. As the name already implies, it means that you simply have to follow the flow or trends. This is a good strategy for a speed option so that you would not miss the trend. However, do not just follow any increase or decrease in value of an underlying asset. Instead, analyze the graph and try to look for a pattern.

➢ Double down

The double down strategy is based on the martingale strategy as used in casino gambling. It is a betting strategy that will allow you to recover all your losses and always make a profit each time you make the right decision. As the name suggests, you simply have to double the amount that you wager every time you encounter a loss. Once you make a winning trade, then you should go back to your base amount (the original amount that you wager). Here is an example: Let us say that you start with $5. If you lose the trade, then your next wager should be $10. Again, if it loses, then wager $20, and so on and so forth. Simply put, just double the wager every time you encounter a loss. If you make the right speculation, then you will be able to recover all of your losses plus a profit. However, take note that options trading does not give back 100%, so you might want to compute the exact amount that you will earn. Be careful; although this may seem like a practical strategy to use, it is also considered highly aggressive. Therefore, use this strategy sparingly.

➢ Conservative betting

This is an excellent betting strategy to use if you are just starting out. But, it is also a good strategy for advanced traders. The key here is to be as conservative as possible. You can do this by using flat betting. It is also advised that you only use a maximum of 2%-3% of your total funds per trade. When you use this approach, you should focus on increasing your success rate. Since you will be using flat betting, you will most likely end up in positive profit provided you maintain a high success rate. To have a high success rate, be sure that every trade that you make is backed up by a solid research.

➢ Mixed

There are also those who suggest that you should not stick to using the same strategy all the time. After all, the market itself does not observe the same behavior all the time. It always changes. The prices of certain assets rise as others fall, and this can continue, but the opposite can also happen. If you use this approach, you can use one strategy for your first trade, and then a different strategy on your next trade and so on. Obviously, this requires more efforts as you will have to learn and practice the different strategies.

> ➢ Asset mastery

The aim of this strategy is to gain mastery over a particular asset. Pick an asset that you want to invest in. Now, make it a priority to read and learn something about that asset every day. After some time, you will have a good understanding of that asset. Learn as much as you can about it. Be sure to spare some time every day to understand the said asset. You will soon notice that you are more able to predict its price movement easily. Once you reach this level, then that is the time for you to use real money and place a wager. Once you gain mastery over a particular asset, then you can jump to another asset. However, remember not to forget about the previous asset/assets that you have mastered.

There is really no such thing as "mastery" of an asset; however, you will know if you are ready to make a real-money trade if you are confident of your understanding of a particular asset. The key to this strategy is gaining more understanding about an asset so that you will be able to speculate its price movement more effectively.

> ➢ Co-integration trading strategy

This strategy relies on the strong correlation between two underlying assets. This usually takes place when two assets belong to the same industry or share the same market.

Due to the high correlation, you will notice that their prices are almost always close to each other. In case there happens to be a significant gap between the prices of the two assets, which usually occurs when one of them has become weak, such gap is only temporary. Due to their high correlation, the prices will adjust again be somewhat close. If you ever notice this, then you are already one step ahead. The only thing left for you to find out now is either to place a *call* on the asset whose price has dropped or a *put* on the asset with a higher price.

> ➢ Corrective

You can use this strategy when you see a sudden surge in price, either a dramatic increase or decrease. Take note that such price spike is only brief and temporary. Soon, the price will balance by returning to its value just before the spike, or at least somewhere close to it. When you see this kind of trend, then you are one step ahead, and you can better make the right trading decision.

> ➢ Make your own

You should realize that you are dealing with a continuously moving and evolving market. So, feel free to come up with your own strategy. You can either develop the strategies that you already know or create something that is totally new. The important thing is that it should work and help rake in positive profits. When you work as a serious trader, it is common to always be working on a strategy. You can expect to do countless of trial and error just to learn and develop an effective strategy. This is simply a normal part of the life of an options trader.

Chapter 4: Keys to Success

✓ Do not chase after your losses

This is a common advice that is given to gamblers, but it also applies when you engage in binary options. "Do not chase after your losses." A quite surprising fact is that those who are well aware of this teaching still fall into this trap. So, how does this work? Chasing after your losses normally happen after you experience a bad loss. The tendency is that you will feel that you have to recover what you have lost and perhaps even profit even by a little. After all, you have already spent time and efforts, so you should at least gain something. However, the problem here is that it tends to change your strategy into an aggressive one. This is because when you chase after your losses, you will have to wager a higher amount since you will take your previous loss into consideration. You will only earn a fixed percentage, so if you want to gain a bigger profit, which would be enough to cover your past loss/losses, then you will have to invest a bigger amount in the next trade. The problem is that there is no amount of research that can guarantee a favorable outcome of a trade. Doing your research and applying the strategies can only increase your chances of making the right trading decision, but they could not guarantee the return of positive profits. So, if you lose your trade again, then just imagine how many losses you will suffer. You should also keep in mind that it is not considered uncommon to experience four, five, or even higher, losing trades in a row, especially if you do not take the time to do all the necessary research and analysis.

This does not mean that chasing after your losses will always end up in a bad way. If you get lucky, you might be able to recover all of your losses and even earn a nice profit. However, the probability of this from happening is quite low. In fact, if you continue to chase after your losses, there is more than a 90% chance that you will end up losing all your funds in the long run due to the highly aggressive approach that it involves. Instead of chasing after your losses, the better advice is to focus on chasing after more profits. Do not allow your losing trades to discourage you. After all, even advanced traders still experience some losing trades every now and then. The important thing is to end up in a positive profit once you add up everything together.

✓ The importance of keeping a journal

Although not considered a requirement, it can still be helpful to write a trading journal. In fact, many expert traders strongly recommend the use of a journal. A trading journal will allow you to view yourself from a new and unbiased perspective. This way, you can more easily identify your strengths and weaknesses. Do not worry; you do not have to be a professional writer to write a trading journal. There are, however, two things that you should always remember: You should update your journal regularly, and you should be honest with everything that you write in your journal.

Your journal should serve as a mirror of yourself. You are free to write everything that you want that is related to your life as an options trader. Ideally, your journal should include your reasons for trading options, your objectives, strategies that you are learning, your expected profit, mistakes and new learnings, and others.

In the first few weeks, you might not appreciate the value of having a journal, but you will soon start to appreciate its importance after some time. Just persist in writing your journal. When you start to see your progress, the more that you will appreciate having a trading journal.

If you are not fond of writing, you may want to use a file on your laptop or even an application on your mobile phone. The important thing is to have a journal where you can record and keep your thoughts and experiences. Also, be sure that your file is secure.

✓ Cash out

Another mistake that beginners often make is not making a withdrawal. Remember that you should cash out your profits from time to time. The reason why some traders only keep their profits in their account is so that they can grow their bankroll or the funds that they use for trading. Although this may seem like a practical reason, it is not a good practice. You should understand that the only way to fully realize your profits is to turn them into real cash, and the way to do that is by making a withdrawal. Do not worry; you can still grow the funds that you use for trading. You do not have to cash out all of your profits right away. If you want, you can just withdraw even just 40% of your profits, leaving the remaining 60% to grow your bankroll. Still, it is important to make a withdrawal every now and then. Cashing out is also an effective way to minimize your risk since the money that you cash out will no longer be lost in any trade. Come to think about it, if you do not make a withdrawal, then it will almost make no difference with managing a mere demo account.

✓ Avoid very quick trades

Avoid wagering on trades as fast as 1 minute or even less. Such timeline may be fun, but it does not reflect the true status of the market. Do not forget that the prices of the different assets continuously fluctuate. Especially if you are a beginner, it is advised to trade using at least the 5-minutes timeframe.

✓ Continuous research and analysis

Keep in mind that you are dealing with a continuously moving market. It is only right that you continue your research and analysis. The assets do not sleep just as the business that holds those assets continue to make progress and developments. Be up to date with the latest trends and analyze the different factors that can affect your investment. Part of this is to continually work on your strategy. Take note that options traders are active traders. You need to be on top of what you do. Since most trades involving options only last for a few minutes, you need to be constantly on the move making analyses and engaging in in-depth research. Take note that the more knowledge and understanding that you have, the greater your chances of making the right trading decision.

✓ Focus on the assets

Looking at the graphs and the charts can make the activity of trading options look sophisticated. Those small numbers on the screen, and those moving lines and stark colors, these are the things people want to see. They will make you think that you understand how to trade just by looking at these visual tools. However, you should understand that this is not enough. When you engage in options trading, you have to focus on the assets themselves and the businesses. Although you can still find patterns by relying on graphs, such is not enough. After all, these patterns do not always happen. And many times, the patterns are impossible to notice in the beginning. And even if you see them, there is no assurance that the trend will not change.

Focus on the assets. Research and study the assets that you are interested in. Read the news about them and look at the financial statements of their companies, as well as related businesses.

✓ Start small

If you are just starting out, it is strongly recommended that you start small. This means that you should keep your wagers low. When you are a beginner, your objective is not to make money right away. Instead, you should first familiarize yourself with the actual trading environment. In fact, it is advised that you should take advantage of a demo account first so that you will not be risking any real money. Once you have developed a good strategy, then you can easily add more funds and increase the amount that you trade with.

The term "small" is still a relative term. A good rule of thumb is to divide your funds by 100. This way you will have to commit 100 wrong decisions before your funds get exhausted.

✓ Diversify

In business, it is taught that you can effectively lower your losses by spreading your risk. The same principle applies when you engage in options trading. You should not wager all of your funds in a single trade. Instead of putting everything in a single trade, you can spread out your funds into multiple trades. Now, a common mistake is to become careless and take some of your trades for granted. Normally, this happens when you get lazy and stop doing enough research. You should always remember that it is better for you not to make a trade than to enter a trade without enough preparation.

✓ Use more than one strategy

It is strongly suggested that you apply at least two strategies. Every strategy will reveal something about a particular asset. As you already know, the more information that you have about an asset the more likely that you will be able to predict its price movement. The more strategies you are able to use, the better. However, you are not expected to use too many strategies as the price behavior of an asset can change quickly. By the time you finish your analysis, then the asset concerned might have already changed its behavior. So, stick to using just two or three strategies to back up your decisions. Experts strongly advise that you should always make use of fundamental analysis as it is the strategy that directly deals with the fundamentals. It is noteworthy that you have not applied fundamental analysis in just one day. Rather, you should follow on the news and be updated on the different assets on a daily basis.

✓ Money management

Even if you have an excellent strategy, you may end up with a negative profit if you do not know how to manage your funds properly. Be careful with how much you are risking and keep a close eye on your losses. You should focus on increasing your profits while minimizing your expenses. Remember not to spend the money that you cannot afford to lose. Also, when you manage your money, you should be as conservative with your expectations. Instead of expecting to double your funds in a day, aim to just profit even just by 10%. Be realistic.

   ✓ Take a break

The life of an options trader can be fun and exciting, but it is definitely not without any challenges. In fact, it can be tiring in the long run, especially if you properly do all the necessary research and preparation.

When you take a break, be sure to use it for relaxation. Do not use it to think about your trading strategies or anything that has to do with options trading. Remember that by giving your body enough time to rest and clearing your mind, you will be more able to think more effectively and come up with good trading decisions. Do not worry; you are expected to work more after the break. You have to learn how to making time for work as well as for rest. Options trading is a long journey. It simply does not end. So, be sure to take some rest every now and then. However, do not use this as an excuse for being lazy. Before you take a rest, you have to render some serious work first.

Chapter 5: Common Mistakes to Avoid

✗ Being an emotional trader

Although it is good to have a passion for what you do, it is not good if you allow your emotions to cloud your judgment. Never allow your emotions to direct your course of action. Instead, every trade has to be backed up by a solid research and analysis. A good way not to be too emotionally attached to your trades is by not spending the money that you cannot afford to lose. Therefore, do not use the money that you need to cover your household bills and other obligations. If you use the money that you cannot afford to lose, it is impossible not to be emotionally attached to your trades. When this happens, you will not be able to think clearly, and this is not good for you as an options trader. If, at any moment, you notice your emotions are influencing your mind, then stop and give your emotions just enough time to settle down. Once you can think more clearly, then that is the time when you can enter a trade, but never enter any trade if you are controlled by your emotions. Usually, people get controlled by their emotions after they experience a losing trade. The problem here is that your emotions might compel you to chase after your losses. You have to learn to control your emotions. Keep in mind that you are dealing with a market that does not care about you. In fact, it does not even know your name. Be objective and reasonable at all times just as the market is not driven by emotions.

✗ Relying on expert advice

When you are a beginner, the tendency is to rely on the pieces of advice given by experts. You might rely on what websites and articles say about options trading. Although this may be good for beginners as far as becoming familiar with options trading is concerned, you should aim to develop your own understanding and view of options trading. It is also worth noting that many of these people who claim to be "experts" are not real experts. In fact, many of these so-called "experts" might even have more losses than profits. After all, these days, it is very easy to promote oneself as an expert with just a few clicks of a mouse, especially if you know how to take advantage of the power of social media. Also, even the real experts out there still commit mistakes from time to time, so always take whatever you read or learn with a grain of salt.

×   Not developing your strategy

Do not forget that you are dealing with a continuously moving market. As such, you also have to keep on developing your strategy. Depending on what happens in the market, the prices of different assets can change their behavior.

Another common mistake is not testing your strategy. You should understand that a slight change in a strategy can have a strong impact on your overall strategy. This is why you always have to test your strategy several times even if you only make slight changes. This is a good time for you to take advantage of the demo account as provided by your broker.

×   Being too aggressive

Avoid being too aggressive. There is no way to completely guarantee the success of a trade. Although it can be tempting to wager a very high amount to get a higher return, it is also a quick way to lose your money. Instead, focus on making small and consistent profits. You should put more emphasis on increasing your success rate. Especially if you are a beginner, it is not good to use any aggressive approach. Start out small and put all your focus on increasing your success rate.

×   Short-term trades

It is common to see a trading period that lasts only for 30 seconds or a minute. Although this looks tempting, it is not advisable that you engage in such very short-term trades, unless if you are sure that the trading platform that you use is 100% trustworthy. The reason is that unscrupulous brokers take undue advantage of the short timeline. Usually, when you engage in a short trade, the value of the asset does not fluctuate that much. You may get the right option as much as the official record is concerned, but you would lose the wager. This is because there is a lapse of a few seconds for the platform to record the updated numbers, and these numbers are being continuously updated. This little delay can cost you your whole wager. Fortunately, not all platforms are like this. There are still reputable and reliable binary trading platforms out there. There are also strategies that are not meant for quick trades. For example, fundamental analysis is not a good strategy to use if you will just trade using a 1-minute timeline because it is not enough time to reflect the status of the market.

✗ Being a victim of the gambler's fallacy

The gambler's fallacy has caused many gamblers and investors to lose all their money. This is something that you should understand. So, what is the gambler's fallacy? It refers to the maturity of chances. The best way to explain it is by using an example. Let us say that in a coin flip, the head side came up four times in a row. What are the chances that the next coin flip will still be a head? Many people would think that the fifth coin flip will most probably be the tail side since head came up many times already. So, people will wager on the tail side. This is the gambler's fallacy. The truth is that even if the head side came up in four consecutive rows, the chances that the fifth coin flip will still be a head is still 50-50. Applying this in options trading, it means that even if *Call* comes five times in a row, it does not mean that the sixth trade that you will make will most likely be a *Put*. Now, you should also take into consideration that options trading is not supposed to be a gamble. The outcome of a trade does not come from a shuffled deck of cards or a random spin of a wheel. To increase your chances of making the right trading decision, you should do all the necessary research and apply your preferred strategy.

✗ Accepting the bonus

It is common for options trading brokers offer catchy bonuses in order to lure you to sign up and use their trading platform. A bonus may look as good as getting an additional 50% of your original deposit. Hence, if you deposit $100, you will have a total fund of $150 in your trading account. Although the bonus may look attractive, it does not come without a catch. The catch is that you will most probably be required to wager around forty times the bonus that you receive before you can make a withdrawal. The problem here is that before you meet the wagering requirement, you will most probably already lose your funds. The tendency is that in order to meet the wagering requirements, you will have to wager a much higher amount than usual. This will turn your strategy into an aggressive strategy, and your bankroll might not be ready for it. Of course, if you are able to devise a strategy that can satisfy the wagering requirement that normally comes with accepting the bonus, then you might want to take advantage of the bonus money.

✗ Superstitious bets

There are some traders who make trades based on mere superstition. For example, a trader who wages all his funds in one trade on his birthday. Although there is nothing wrong with believing in superstition, you should not use it as a basis for making a trade. The market does not care about superstitions. Instead, you should study the asset that you want to trade. This way, you will have a better chance at making the right trading decision instead of merely relying on superstitions.

✗ Trading as a hobby

There are many people who start trading options as a hobby. Although there is nothing wrong with this approach, it is not the recommended way to trade binary options. This is because trading as a mere hobby signifies lack of dedication, seriousness, and commitment. Instead of trading as a hobby, it is advised that you should approach trading as you would a business or any other profession. If you cannot give it enough time, then just be a part-time trader. This is better than not taking it seriously. You should understand that real and successful option traders take their work seriously. In fact, this is how they make continuous profits. They read numerous data and make solid research on a regular basis. They do not just consider it as a hobby, but they know just how important every trade is. Options trading is not supposed to be happy. If you want to achieve access, then it is time for you to be more serious about it by considering it to be some form of business or profession.

   ✗ Not knowing when to stop

It is not uncommon to find traders who spend hours on their computer studying certain assets. Many times, they get too caught up in what they are doing that they do not notice the time. Just as you should know when to make a trade, you should also know when to call it a day and take some rest. Although generally, anyone above 18 years of age can start to trade options, this activity is not for everyone. If you notice that trading options continuously make you lose more money, then learn to stop, even just temporarily.

However, if you are quite stubborn to persist despite so many losses, then you might want to shift to making only small wagers until you develop a more effective strategy. Now, just as you should know when to stop when you encounter a series of losses, you should also know when to stop when you experience many successful trades.

It is not uncommon to find traders who enjoy significant profits, but only to encounter big and continuous losses after a while. This is another reason why you better withdraw your profits before you hit the ceiling.

   ✗ Compulsive trading

This is like emotional trading. However, in this case, you just want to feel that you are still in the game. This is where you make trades even if you do not see any good opportunities to make a profit. Remember to only make a wager if you are confident of your position. Do not take any trade for granted.

Instead of submitting to this impulse, you should control yourself and focus on doing more research as you observe proper timing.

× Greed

Greed is something that you should definitely watch out for. Greed has led many traders to lose their money. It is hard to stop greed since you cannot see or touch it. It appears as a strong impulse inside you that compels you to desire more profits to the point that you can become careless. In order to avoid the consequences of being greedy, you should have a plan. It is good if you can come up with a short-term plan and a long-term plan. This way you will always have a good sense of direction no matter what happens to a trade. If, at any moment, you feel like you are being controlled by greed, then stop whatever it is that you are doing, do not make any trade, and just allow the strong impulse to settle down. After some time, you will be more able to think more clearly and take appropriate actions.

Chapter 6: The Successful Trader's Mindset

Your mindset is very important when you engage in options trading. Without the right mindset, you will most likely fail to make the right trading decisions. Let us examine how a successful trader thinks so that you will have an idea of how you should cultivate yourself as an options trader:

- Study and practice

Since you are dealing with a moving and living market, it is only right that you continue studying it. Many changes can happen in a day. There are also so many factors that affect the price movements of different assets. As an options trader, you should study the different theories and strategies and you should also continue practicing what you know. Do not forget that being a successful options trader is not all about theories—you also need to learn how to put your knowledge into actual practice. Study and practice should be a normal part of your daily routine as a trader.

- Self-discipline

As an options trader, everything depends on your decisions. Hence, you are also responsible for all of your actions. This is the kind of life where you are in control of everything. At the same time, you are responsible for everything. You have to exercise self-discipline. Every professional and successful trader knows that it takes hard and serious work to be a successful trader, especially if you want to remain successful for a long period of time. You have to stick to doing lots of research and render in-depth analysis of different underlying assets. In the beginning, it may be hard to impose discipline on yourself, but you have to realize how important being disciplined is. From time to time, you will have to force yourself to do research and analysis. You cannot afford to be lax and lazy. You cannot depend on anyone else for success but yourself. After some time, you will get used to the level of discipline that is required of professional traders. It is just really not that simple to change habits, but it is nonetheless doable.

- Calm

Successful traders are always calm. They are calm even when others are already panicking. They know that they should not allow themselves to be controlled by their emotions, and so they remain calm so that they could think more effectively. They do not panic even when they lose a trade because they have realized that losing some trades is a natural part of the game. After all, there is no amount of preparation that can guarantee a favorable outcome. However, this does not mean that you should no longer do your research. Remember that by doing research and analysis, you can significantly increase your chances of making the right trading decision and earning a nice profit. If you feel like you are losing your calm, then just relax and stop thinking about anything that has to do with options trading. Instead, just calm down and wait until you can think more objectively again. Sometimes all that you need to do is not to take any action and just wait.

- Open yet reasonable

Professional traders have an open mind. This is how they are able to come up with interesting ideas on how they can take advantage of certain assets. However, do not fall into the pitfall of being too open that you are led to believe something that is no longer possible. Remember to be open, but you should also stick to good reasons. Make sure that every trade that you make is backed up by solid research.

- Objective

Remain objective at all times. Do not forget that you are dealing with assets that do not feel any kind of emotion. You have to think rationally. Although it is good to sometimes daydream by focusing on the fruits of your actions, you should realize that it is more important to focus on the actions themselves. Do not be like the others who get too caught up in the outcome that they fail to take positive actions to actually make things happen.

- Patient

Successful traders are patient. Make sure to observe the proper timing. When it comes to timing, patience is important. Do not commit the common mistake of trading options during an unstable time or when it is hard to predict the price movements of assets. Learn to wait. Indeed, you will soon notice that there are times when you are able to speculate the price movements of different assets more easily, but there are also times when no matter what you do it would seem that you cannot predict how certain assets will behave. Be patient and make a trade only when you are confident of your decision.

- Not attached to their money

Professional and successful traders are not attached to the money that they can earn. Instead of being too busy thinking about how much you can earn, spend your time and efforts on learning the best strategy to use and how you can execute it more effectively. Realize that money will come on its own as long as you take the right actions.

- Persistent

Successful traders did not start out with a success story right away. In fact, most of them have encountered many losses before they truly learned to be an excellent trader. This is part of the journey to becoming a highly successful options trader. The important thing is for you not to give up. You should keep on trying despite many difficulties. The more that you take positive actions, the more you will learn and improve as a trader.

The mindset of a successful trader may not be easy to achieve right away. Again, persistence is the key. You need to give yourself time to adjust and adapt to a new way of thinking. After some time, you will get used to this kind of mindset that it will all be just second nature to you.

Conclusion

Thanks for making it through to the end of this book. We hope it was informative and able to provide you with all of the tools you need to achieve your goals whatever they may be.

The next step is to apply everything that you have learned and start raking in serious profits. Keep in mind that learning how to trade options effectively requires more than reading books. It is also a skill that needs to be developed. If you are just starting out, remember to start small or better yet, just stick first to using a demo account. Learning how to trade options effectively can create a strong positive impact on your life. However, options trading also has its own challenges and obstacles that you must overcome. By understanding and following the teachings in this book and practicing the strategies, you will be able to turn the options trading market into a goldmine of profits.

Finally, if you found this book useful in any way, a review on Amazon is always appreciated!

54523493R00144